THE PROFIT SYSTEM'S FATE

BY

CLIFFORD L. KERNS

SECOND EDITON

Revised and retitled edition of
Common Sense Economics, March, 1993

ISBN 978-0-7414-0145-8

Printed in the United States of America

Published December 1999

INFINITY PUBLISHING

Toll-free (877) BUY BOOK
Local Phone (610) 941-9999
Fax (610) 941-9959
Info@buybooksontheweb.com
www.buybooksontheweb.com

PREFACE

In a first time use of system law to analyze our economic system, this book forms a cause and effect basis to predict that the profit process can not endure.

What should you do after reading the above statement? It is difficult to believe that the economic system we have used for more than 200 years could be doomed by its basic process. Your life is involved, so it is wise to read the analysis yourself to determine truth.

Our economic system is tottering badly. Beware of placing all blame on the operators of the system. You would be fooling yourself. The mathematics of the profit process works towards system failure regardless of competence or ignorance of politicians and rich people. For instance, the profit process makes it impossible to pay the national debt which is bankrupting us.

There can be no surenesss of individual survival unless it is supported by group survival for the great mass of people. There can be no expectations of group survival unless it is supported by mass awareness of true economic cause and effect, and awareness of impending self destruction of the profit system.

The great mass of people must become aware of the absolute need to build a replacement non profit, non dictatorial economic and social system. Survival rests on this awareness.

CONTENTS

Chapter 1.
Single Business Profit System

This is a very serious book about economic systems. Maybe it will seem strange to you that the first thing we will talk about is cookies. Almost all four year old children could tell you that you can not take more cookies out of a cookie jar than there are cookies in the jar. This is the first law of all systems. You can not take more out of any system than there is in it.

We presently use the profit system as our main way to produce and distribute. During some indefinite period, people invest 100 billion dollars and expect to get back 110 billion. The basic law of systems tells us that we can not put 100 billion into the system and take out 110 billion. Yet at the present time, investors are taking more money out of the system than they are putting into it. This seems like a contradiction. We observe the profit system working, seemingly in spite of system law.

We need to look further if we wish to explain the seeming contradiction. Let's assume we give a fourth grade child a piece of paper and a pencil. We ask the child to draw a kindergarten style sailboat.

"Mary, here is a penny to pay you for making the sailboat. I own it now, and wish to sell it. Let us act like you wish to buy this sailboat picture."

"O.K.," says Mary. "How much do you want for it?"

"I want two pennies so that I can make a profit," I tell her.

"But," says Mary, "I only have one penny. I can't buy the sailboat." Kids tend to have clear vision if it is about something in their experience.

"I will let you sign an IOU for one penny. With the penny you earned plus the one penny IOU you can buy the sailboat picture," I tell Mary. The deal is completed. Note that by using debt, both production and distribution has been accomplished.

Aha! We have begun to explain what seemed like contradiction between cookie jar law and the 110 billion dollar return on a 100 billion dollar investment. A profit system demands a "money" increase or it will not work. Let us reword that statement, and call it the law of the profit system. Enough buying power must be injected into the system to allow profit or else the system fails.

This conclusion slipped up on us so easily it may be hard to recognize its great importance. Using cookie jar law, we have found a direct cause and effect explanation of how either prosperity or depressions occur.

You are likely disturbed because IOUs were used as the money increase in our sailboat example. How about gold? Or silver? Diamonds?

Following centuries of custom, money was raw gold, raw silver, or coins made from gold or silver. A person was rich if he found enough gold or silver. A nation was rich if enough gold or silver was found within the nation. When our nation was young and tiny, the finding of gold and silver increased the money enough that the profit system worked. During the last 100 years, finding of gold and silver has been far less than needed for prosperity.

Growth of great quantities of IOUs, or debt, has been needed to enable operation of the profit system. Strangely, debt such as IOUs is often used as money. That is why IOUs were used in the sailboat example. The seeming contradiction of a profit system working contrary to system law is explained by debt increase.

Using system law as a tool, you can find cause and effect explanations for countless profit system conditions. Those explanations may be very unlike those you have learned before. We will cover a few.

If you brought a stack of college economics text books home from a book store, not one book would cover the cookie jar law of systems. Not one would derive the cause and effect idea that a profit system can not work unless buying power increases enough to pay profit. During 200 years, many stories have tried to explain operation of capitalism, which is what people often call our profit system. Those stories fall short because they fail to apply the right approach, which is use of system law to analyze the basic profit system process.

Conclusions in those books are based on coincidence. Reasoning by coincidence may be correct, but also is often wrong, like the four year old girl who told her mother, "Each time I put my pajamas on, it makes it get dark outside." Using system law in our study of the profit system, we can be free of errors caused by using coincidence. We have a solid cause and effect basis to predict whether or not the profit system can last permanently. That prediction is our first major goal in this book.

Now that the first direction of this book has been pointed out, let's use several practice examples to apply what has been learned, leading towards prediction of what will come.

In our early example, we allowed Mary to use IOUs to buy a sailboat picture, saying that debt increase made the profit process work. Our very simple example shows what might be called a single business profit system. What happens if we repeat production and sale steps many times?

Let's again use the sailboat picture example. "Mary," I may say, "several times now, you have drawn a picture of a sailboat. Each time, I have allowed you to use the penny I paid you and an IOU to buy the sailboat picture. You have lots of pictures now, but all I have is my original penny and several IOUs. Let us stop producing sailboats until you have paid me pennies for those IOUs."

"But," Mary protests, "I don't have any pennies at all. Also, if you no longer hire me to draw sailboats, I can never earn any more pennies. I can not pay my debt." This shows that in a single business system, repeated investment gives only a stack of IOUs as profit. You can not stop production as a way of turning IOUs into cash. IOUs are not deferred cash profit. We have production and distribution time after time only if credit continues. When credit ceases, production and distribution stops. Depression and a stack of useless IOUs result. The obvious instability of this process can hardly escape our notice.

Another way in which unsatisfactory operation of the profit system shows up is accumulation of unsold goods in warehouses. "George," I tell a fourth grader, "I paid you a penny to draw a sailboat picture. You want it, but you can't buy it from me at a price of two cents. You are "laid off" until I can sell the picture to you." But if George could not buy the picture when he was employed, it will remain unsold after he no longer has a job.

Unsold goods piling up in warehouses at a time of growing unemployment makes a strange paradox. There is abundance of goods during a time when unemployed people suffer because they can not buy the unsold goods. When these goods begin to accumulate in large quantities, many people call them overproduction and think that stopping production for a time will allow the goods to be sold. Both ideas are fallacies. When people are in need, an unsaleable surplus is not overproduction. Unemployed workers can not buy the unsold abundance.

Inflation has a very strong effect on the operation of a profit system. Let's use another of our fourth grader stories. "Mary," I say, "last time you were paid one penny for drawing a sailboat picture. You bought the picture from me using the newly earned penny plus a one penny IOU. This time labor costs are up so I will pay you two cents. To buy the picture from me, you will have to give me two pennies and a two cent IOU."

We can easily see that money has become worth only one half as much as it was before. A price rise reduces the effectiveness of money. Let's emphasize a point. The price rise during inflation lowers effective money in an economic system which demands a money increase to operate. Using slang wording, this is a double whammy. Inflation can quickly bring about depression.

This cause and effect result of inflation is easy to understand. When people see their economy slump as inflation destroys the value of money, how can they miss seeing that a profit system always demands a money increase? Real understanding of profit system operation is "very close to the surface" when inflation accentuates our view of the basic system, yet people miss the idea.

Many people seem to know that the law of supply and demand is a close cause of inflation. This long known economics law says that the seller can get a higher price as the goods he sells get scarcer and a lower price as the goods become more abundant. That is about half of the law. If buyers have plenty of money, the seller can get higher prices than if buyers have little money. Some people would say that buyer's desires control prices, but desires don't mean much without money to back them. The supply of money is the control. We should note that only during the direst times do the prices descend below a lower limit. Prices seem to hold not lower than the cost of the items.

Yet, what people try to do affects prices and inflation. Let's think about real estate lots in a city. When real estate is bought by a person who intends to resell at a profit he raises the price then waits for a buyer. This speculative investment depends upon inflation, and also helps to cause it. If 1000 real estate speculators each buy a lot one day, the price of all lots in the city are higher next day. If this process is done several times more, it assures the inflation on which the investor depends. Also, if prosperity prevails, the process tends to be one way, and that is to higher prices. As long as credit extension is condoned, giving prosperity, prices rise.

The wage-price spiral also feeds inflation, as we saw in our "fourth grader" example. When prices increase, the wage earner's pay buys less. If the wage earners push enough, their pay is raised. However, the busines owner is then forced to ask a higher price for his goods. This cancels the wage earner's pay raise. The whole process is like a dog chasing its tail, with "cost of living" increases causing higher "cost of living." Long acceptance of this has made it seem "normal."

The examples just covered show that what people do effects operation of our economic system, but people's actions are limited by arithmetic working inside of system law. These few examples we have touched on only scratch the surface, but show how easily we can understand the operation of our economic system if we take the system law approach.

Before we look at multi business profit systems, here is a review of ideas that apply to a single business profit system. These ideas show rough relationships between cost, profit, sale price, and market. In a single business (monopoly) profit system, the market equals the investment. Profit is not possible. Pure slavery used as an attempt to make 100 percent profit doesn't give any profit. Zero wages gives a zero market. If an investor pays his full sale price to acquire goods for sale, then his market is 100 percent, but his profit is zero. The ratio of the market created by a merchant depends upon what portion of his sale price is paid to purchase or produce goods.

As we close this first chapter, the most important and universal idea is that you can not take more out of a system than there is in it. The second most important idea is that buying power must be endlessly inserted into a profit system or the profit system ceases to function. The insights and conclusions formed in this chapter will be our compass to steer through study of a multi business profit system, and beyond.

Chapter 2.
Multi Business Profit System

Because we were only considering a single business profit system in Chapter 1, you may feel prone to discard Chapter 1 ideas as unimportant. The examples and conclusions may seem to be mere bedtime stories, not applicable to the complex multi business profit system we have used on a national basis since prerevolutionary war days. Do not go astray. The insights and conclusions apply and are binding in any profit system, simple or complex.

In spite of some depressions since the United States became a nation, our multi business profit system has furnished our nation the highest living standard in the world. Looking back at this much success, it might seem certain that a multi business profit system will permanently work.

You might easily drive a new automobile 30,000 miles with no tire trouble. Yet you would not expect 130,000 trouble free miles from the tires just because they lasted 30,000 miles. If I told you that our economic system might fail after working 200 years you would likely say we should not compare tires to a multi business profit system. Tires wear, but an economic system such as ours might grow better. Yet, based only on its past record you would not be right to assume either failure or success of our profit system during the next 200 years. However, if we apply and expand knowledge learned in Chapter 1, we should be able to predict the future behavior of our multi business profit system.

Using very simple examples and system law, let us begin study of multi business profit system operations.

Let's imagine three tiny profit system businesses on an island. We can let their procedures and goals copy those typical of business. The island setting, with no outside trade, will be our system. This should make it easy to follow multi business activity. After looking at real simple operations, we can add complexities, like banking, govenmental debt and spending, taxation, and so on.

One of the businesses on the island will be a brick making plant. Brick clay on the island will be used. A second business can be a furniture factory and sales outlet. Trees on the island will be used for the furniture. A third business will be a farm, growing and selling food. You know, of course, that these three businesses could not furnish the complete needs of a community. We will ignore this fact because we only need to trace the flow of money and goods as the three businesses strive to make profit.

The brick plant owner invests $100 by paying his workers to make bricks which have a sale price of $110. The furniture factory owner has $110 worth of furniture made by paying $100 to his employees. The farmer pays $100 to his field people and expects to sell the produce for $110.

A bit of addition tells us there is a $300 pool of buying power if we agree there is no money except the investment money. Continuing to add, you can tell that the sale price of all newly produced goods is $330. Subtraction shows that the buying power of consumers falls $30 short of the total sale price of the goods. You can state that in a multi business profit system, buying power distributed during investment is less than the sale price of the goods arising from the investment. The short fall equals the hoped for profit. Also, unsold goods equal hoped for profit.

Cookie jar law shows us that everything true for a single business is also true for a multi business system. You can't take more out of a jar than there is in it, even with three or more businesses. You may begin to feel that we have disclosed a very serious problem faced by the profit system.

As we let sales begin, you know that only $300 worth can be bought by consumers, and that $30 worth will remain unsaleable. The furniture merchant sells all his goods and receives $110. The farmer/grocer is also successful. Can we tell in advance how many dollars worth of bricks the consumers can buy? Of course. The brick yard owner can sell $80 worth of bricks, and must retain $30 worth. Do the arithmetic to gain understanding.

You see that the furniture merchant and the farmer/grocer were able to each make $10 profit, but their profit caused a $20 loss in investment money for the brick yard owner.

Many economists, and perhaps other people, have praised "free market" competition. They talk about how competition between businesses that are alike keep prices down and product quality up. Both of these results of competition are said to benefit the consumer. Yet, looking at competition from the cookie jar viewpoint yields a surprise.

From the system law approach, we see that three totally different kinds of business are competing with each other for a $300 buying power pool. When two of these different kinds of business successfully withdraw $220 from the money pool, the third kind of business, the brick business, suffers investment loss while also holding unsaleable surplus goods. There has been severe competition, not between like kind of businesses, but between unlike businesses. The brick yard owner may be forced out of business. His employees may suddenly find that they are unemployed. To summarize, a profit system business is in competition with those of all other kinds.

This shows how the success of a grocery store in some town can be "wiping out" a jewelry store even though it is the only jewelry store in town. A copper mining town in Upper Michigan can be entering very hard times when grocery stores in Ohio drain the buying power pool during periods of insufficient national money increase.

Shall we return to the brick yard and the imaginary island? The $30 worth of bricks that are unsaleable occur in a multi business profit system. We can say that in a multi business profit system, as in single business, there is an unsaleable surplus of goods equal in price to the total profit expected within the system. This surplus is not necessarily overproduction. Rather, it simply is inability of a profit system to distribute all of the goods that can be produced. To needy people, no goods are no goods, whether from inability to produce or from inability to distribute. During the 1929 Great Depression, vast stores of unsaleable goods glutted warehouses while 13 million unemployed, and their families, were in dire need.

Shall we allow the furniture maker/merchant to buy $10 worth of bricks from the brick yard? He can use the $10 profit he has made. He need not dip into his investment, his capital, to buy bricks. If he does buy $10 worth of bricks, the brick yard owner's investment loss drops to $10. The brick yard owner's $30 unsaleable brick surplus drops to $20 worth. He may become optimistic about business and not close his brick yard.

This sounds promising. It implies that if all business owners who make profit will merely spend all their profit as consumers, the profit system might work as a result. In short, heavy consumerism by investors might mean they are not trying to take more money out of the system than they put into it. We need not force them. We must naturally expect investors to be consumers, too. In investor consumerism, haven't we found the magic wand by which the profit system can work inside the confines of system law?

Hold back your euphoria. The furniture maker/merchant in our example would indeed be expected to "eat up his profit" sometimes. "Sometimes" hardly qualifies an action as normal. We must also consider a word called capitalism. Normal capitalistic procedure excludes "eating up one's profit." The normal attempt is to save profit and include it into future investment. The furniture merchant invested $100. He sold all his furniture, getting $110 return on his $100 investment. Next time around, normally, he would invest $110 in the making of still more furniture. The sale price of this second round of production could likely be $121, expecting a ten percent profit. This is the process of capitalism. Note that capitalism is more than making profit. It is mainly using profit to enlarge one's original investment.

How, then, do we "feed" the investors? A factory owner simply pays himself a salary which is included alongside of his worker's wages as part of the investment to get production. Other business owners pay themselves a salary in the same way, hoping to keep all profit to increase future investment. Refusing to "eat up profit" means that investor consumerism is NOT a magic wand by which endlessly sought profit is cancelled, by which the profit system does not try to take more out of a system than is in it.

The profit system mathematically demands that money be added. In a single business system, IOUs endlessly stacking up seemed the only way to add the neccessary money. However, the investor, recognizing the endless IOUs as fake profit, would halt more credit. Yet, as we search for a way for the multi business profit system to work continuously, the only way seems to be endless increase of IOUs, or debt. We can be sure that this debt can not accumulate in the hands of the investor or he will stop business. People got around this problem by passing debt on, to be carried by someone other than the investor.

One group that IOUs could be passed onto has been banker people. An even bigger group that has carried the huge present day debt load is the government. We can not easily keep the direct simplicity of the three business island as we study the role of banks and government in the endless growth of debt. We will keep our story as simple as possible, but you will have to be careful that no faulty analogies are made.

Turning back to the start of our three business system, we see that the brick yard owner had an $80 return on his $100 investment. The furniture merchant and the grocer each had a $110 return on their investments, and no surplus goods to sell. The brick yard owner still had $30 worth of bricks, a loss of $20, and was ready to shut down his brick plant because of depression. Shut down would bring unemploymnet. We will continue, now. First we will agree that we can now have more than $300 on the island. Let us assume that the government on the island decides it can use $30 worth of bricks.

The government votes to create a government bond, (a very fancy IOU), for $30. It sells the bond to the bank, then uses the $30 from the bank to buy bricks. The brick yard owner is very happy about the sudden upturn of business. There will be no depression. For a short time, government spending based on debt seems to have rescued the economy.

We can see why business likes to have government carry the credit load. The investor does not have to grant credit in order to sell his goods. The investor is not left holding non-cashable IOUs. The government bond, (an IOU), may be put out of mind by the investor, and prosperity can exist. However, the bond is something you are aware of.

You do a bit of accounting and know that the government went into debt by the amount which gave the three businesses continued prosperity. You look a bit closer. You discover that the bank expects to charge 10 percent interest on the loan it made when it "bought" the $30 government bond. The bank will allow the government to take the bond back someday for $33, so the debt is not merely $30. You are now aware that the island no longer has just three businesses. The bank is an investor, and there are four profit making businesses on the island.

You continue to complete the circle. The government is of the people, by the people, and for the people. The government is expected to tax the people of the island when bricks are bought for the people. We conclude that the government extended prosperity when it used an IOU to buy $30 worth of bricks. But if the government taxes people $33 to get the bond back from the bank, prosperity will fall flat on its face. Buying power will not have been increased within the island profit system, and that system demands an increase of buying power to continue to work.

Read very, very slowly for a bit so that you can think hard and long about the impossibility of taxing people to pay off our 5 1/2 trillion dollar national debt. National political and financial leaders think it can be done.

Your author must confess to you that he gets jittery along about this stage of the story. The jitters arises from observing the massiveness of farce and self deception that people tolerate. However, in defense of people, they have been born into the multi business profit system, banks, governmental spending, and taxation by government. I am going to coin a great white-washing quotation. "Whatever the pattern of life is that we get used to, from childhood to adulthood, we later tend to think of that pattern as the only correct one."

You will perhaps come up with an idea about using endless growth of governmental debt as a way of giving endless prosperity. Looking back two paragraphs, we see that if the government taxed people $33, the buying power increase that had enabled prosperity would be more than cancelled. You say, "What if we instruct our government to issue money to give our profit system the money increase it must have for prosperity?"

As you think about this idea, you may think about government bonds, IOUs, and the nature of money. It is probably time for more talk about money, since you may be thinking of some way to endlessly increase it. For example, through all this book, IOUs have been talked about as being buying power. Yet, we know that IOU means debt. It means a very brief contract: "I Owe You" some amount. Long standing custom makes IOU also mean "I Promise To Pay You." IOU means that the person who granted credit or made a loan gets in his possession a written note to prove that you owe him. How, then, can these IOUs be buying power, especially when we speak of allowing IOUs to endlessly accumulate as a way to enable production and distribution in a profit system?

Money is anything which people agree is money. (Boy, what a dodge.) We are not really stepping off into quicksand with the statement made above. We are all familiar with a dollar bill. If someone has a loaf of bread and I have a dollar (coin or paper), the dollar is money because I can exchange it for the bread. The person selling the bread agrees with me that the dollar is money. He, in turn, expects every one else to agree the dollar is money when he uses it to buy something.

People native to the Pacific Islands area once used large sea shells as money. The North American Indians made tiny beads from shells, wove the beads into patterns, called it wampum, and used it as a means of exchange, or money, to avoid physical barter. Genghiz Khan, about the year 1225, had conquered huge areas of Mongolia, China, and India. He had metal disks made to be money. The coins were about the same size, same material, but quite different in value depending on symbols pressed into the metal faces. Those coins helped unify and ease commerce in his vast empire. The coins also, and note this, were first spent by the government. This seems to have averted taxation in his day. Perhaps entirely unknown to Genghiz Khan, the low demand profit system of his day was also aided greatly by money increase. I say the coins were one percent solid bronze and ninety nine percent solid confidence.

Now if we feel that money is whatever people agree is money, we can look at many forms today. The IOU examples we used were chosen as a fast method of leading you into the idea that most of our forms of money today really are certificates of debt, but accepted by us so much that they are money. (You can buy a vast amount with the right government bond.)

A very much used present day form of money is the plastic credit card, often called "plastic money." The credit card is really a bank loan that is prearranged, and is an open loan account, an endless "revolving" loan. It is quite different from the old fashioned bank loan, when each loan amount was approved as a single loan. The credit card does not open the loan until the card is used. The accounts are generally paid within a month, or a few months, with new charges "revolving" into the account even as past debt is paid. Even though the time may be short between charges on the card and payment, that time lapse is enough to allow an astonishing amount of debt to pile up. It has been estimated that within the entire nation, there is a daily standing credit card debt of more than one trillion dollars.

With credit cards, a vast number of consumers owe the debt, and many banks and companies hold the IOUs. Banks hold mortgages, automibile liens, and many other kinds of documents to cover a wide variety of debt. There is such a multitude of debt repositories that they can not be counted. There are loans taken out to pay earlier loans, to beat the time factor. There are governmental bonds used to pay for earlier bonds, or just to keep up with interest payments on earlier bonds. People have become adept at hiding debt and delaying payment. All of this debt (money) increase partly buys continuing prosperity.

Governmental debt is probably the main source of money increase. If we would like to instruct our government to increase money to give us endless prosperity, we don't have to find gold first. We could tell our government to print money. However, even though a government print shop could turn out money as needed, there are many problems. Would we have confidence in money printed just to enable profit system success? Who would spend it first? Could we control people who had so much power? What about inflation? Would people agree to all this change? Would banks crash? What would we do if the United States went into debt to increase buying power, but foreign nations reaped all of the benefits?

In addition to the above questions, the hardest problem is a mathematical one. Before we look at it, let's skim over 60 years of history.

Sometime in the 1930's, our nation began a slow one-way increase of governmental debt. The debt spending began to take the nation's profit system out of the 1929 Depression. Before any new depression could occur, the 1940's saw preparation for, and entry into, World War II. Never before had prosperity sat on so large an amount of governmental spending, with a great increase in national debt.

When World War II was finished, the backlog of money from the war years kept prosperity going. Before prosperity got weak, the United States began to drift into what became known as the Cold War against communism. Governmental debt grew until the Cold War ended. In September, 1998, the United States Treasury Dept. reported that the national debt passed five and a half trillion dollars ($5,500,000,000,000). Some people lived well off of the interest on that amount. But of course the profit system had its needed money increase on a continuing basis. That pattern takes us to 1998 with no depression.

Before we again take up the pros and cons about endless governmental debt growth, you might tarry a minute to note the stated goal of the Cold War. The United States entered the Cold War to block a way of life known as communism. That way of life was one of very rigid military dictatorship over an economic system which was state owned and operated. During this Cold War, the profit system thrived on our governmental debt spending. Under communism, consumers took a beating, with much production going into armament. The profit system countries looked better to consumers than communist countries did.

Our Cold War prosperity was very predictable, with system law knowledge. And now we want to predict whether or not we can make the profit system permanent. We wonder if we can sustain prosperity by requiring our government to forever continue debt increase, likely without drain of taxation. There would be problems so numerous and so great that life patterns would change. The first need would be universal recognition of the reality of cookie jar law in our economic system. In spite of all contriving, such endless debt increase, such endless governmental spending will run into a mathematical limitation.

To make the mathematical limits obvious, we will use our three business profit system example again. Let's require that the bank and the government on the imaginary island act jointly to increase buying power indefinitely as needed by a profit system. The manner in which governmental debt will have to increase can be shown by an investment followed by an endless string of successful reinvestments. We can simplify the observations by watching the money increase needs of just one of the businesses, such as the furniture bussiness. That one example will show the stages of successful investment and reinvestment. $100 is invested at a profit rate of 10 percent. The $100 becomes $110. This reinvested, at the same profit rate, becomes $121. Again reinvested, the amount becomes $133.10. You most likely are very aware of the arithmetic procedure for computing reinvestment growth.

We are using the long familiar compound interest formula, which mathematically describes the investment and reinvestment process. I would like to make a change in wording though, and call this the compound profit formula. In algebraic form, the formula is $A = I(1+r)$ with exponent n, where A is the accumulative amount when investment I has been reinvested successfully n times at a profit rate r.

Using that formula, starting with $I = \$100$ and $r = 0.1$, we see that a $100 investment becomes $110, then $121, then $133.10, $146.41, $161.05, $177,16, and so on, with an ever greater difference between each next step. I have included some numerical tables and the graphs of compound growth for a few sample rates. Looking at the graphs, you can get a "feel" for the problem of increasing governmental debt over a long time.

Study the table on page 24 and study the graph on page 25. Resume text on page 26.

YRS	GROWTH RATE, PERCENT PER YEAR 2	3	4	5
0	1.00	1.00	1.00	1.00
10	1.24	1.06	1.54	1.71
20	1.52	1.86	2.28	2.79
30	1.85	3.50	3.37	4.32
40	2.25	3.36	4.80	7.04
50	2.75	4.52	7.12	11.47
60	3.35	6.07	10.52	18.68
70	4.08	8.16	15.57	30.43
80	4.97	10.96	23.05	49.56
90	6.06	15.17	34.12	80.73
100	7.39	20.39	50.50	131.50
110	9.01	27.40	74.76	214.20
120	10.98	36.82	110.66	348.91
130	13.38	49.49	163.80	568.34
140	16.32	66.51	242.47	925.77
150	19.89	89.38	358.92	1507.97
160	24.25	120.12	531.29	2456.33
170	29.55	161.44	786.44	4001.10
180	36.03	216.96	1164.12	6517.37
190	43.92	291.57	1723.19	10616.61
200	53.53	391.85	2550.74	17292.51
210	65.26	526.61	3775.72	28167.68
220	79.55	707.72	5588.98	45882.18
230	96.97	951.12	8273.06	74737.23
240	118.21	1278.22	12246.15	121739.04
250	144.09	1717.82	18127.29	198300
260	175.65			
270	214.11			

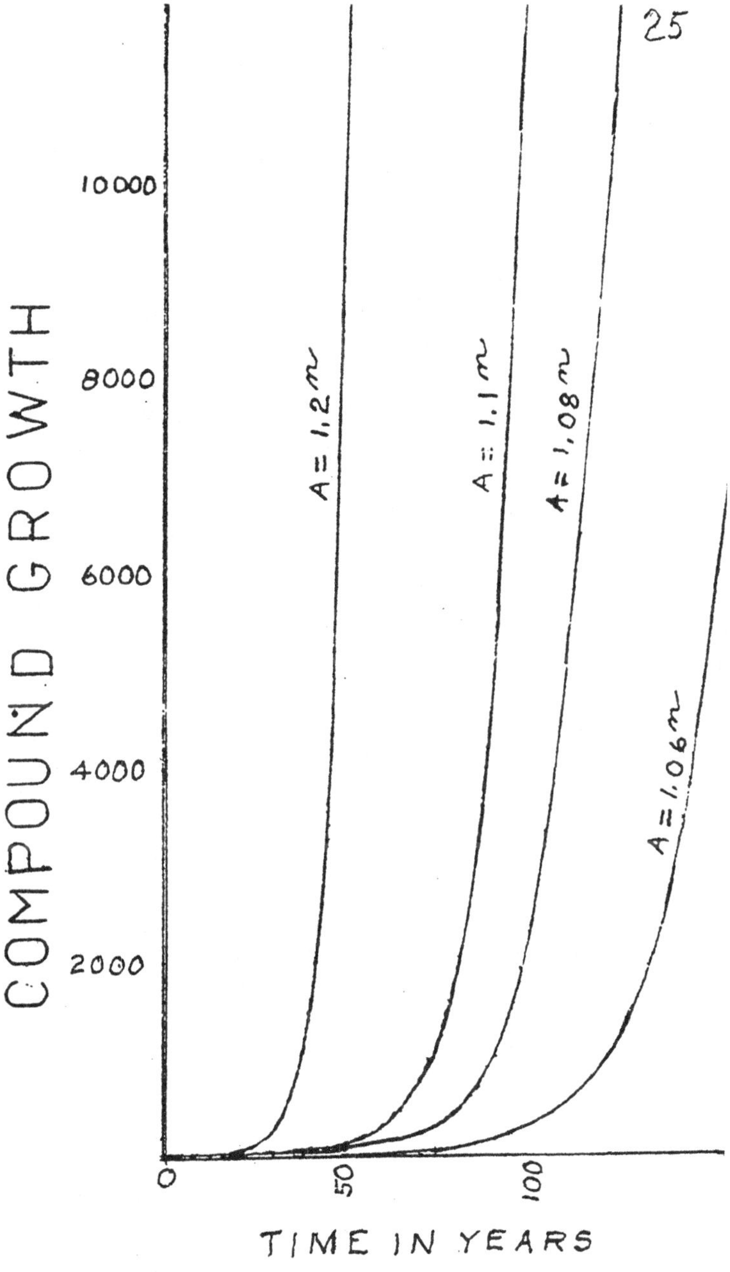
COMPOUND GROWTH
10000
8000
6000
4000
2000
0
50
100
TIME IN YEARS
A = 1.2^n
A = 1.1^n
A = 1.08^n
A = 1.06^n

The table on page 24 shows the amount that one dollar would become if invested at compound interest at the rates indicated as column heads. It also shows the manner in which the national money pool would have to increase to sustain the profit system at any of the profit rates indicated as column heads. The table totally ignores the extra increase needed to cancel inflationary devaluation of money.

The graphs on page 25 gives us a pictoral display showing the growth which we see in the tables.

As you look at the page of tables and the graphs, note the ever larger difference between each ten year step. It is this difference between steps that shows how debt, (buying power), must grow during that ten year period to give further prosperity. When the growth is "young", the difference is small, but when the growth is "mature," we can see that the growth becomes difficult to sustain. Our nation, and our economy are more than 200 years old. We are in the mature stage of compound growth.

The average percent rate of profit during the past 200 years is unknown. It has been extremely variable. We do not have to know which rate column our economy fits best. Looking at the graphs on page 25 we see that each growth pattern reaches a stage where it grows very much like the preceeding curve. Since all percentage rate curves grow so much alike, we only need to note that our economy is over 200 years old. We see the ever increasing increment by which debt must grow as ten year periods follow one another.

We may think that our actual debt does not grow at a fantastic rate, that the curves on page 25 really do not apply. However, a single example shows that between 1945 and 1980, a period of 35 years, the actual increase of the federal debt was 249 percent. In only 10 years between 1980 and 1990, the federal debt grew by 253 percent. The latter decade of growth equalled the preceeding 35 year's growth. Our actual debt does grow at a fantastic rate, and gets worse every year.

In the two years after April, 1990, the United States national debt grew from 3 trillion dollars to almost 4 trillion dollars. This growth in debt was enough at that time to bring recovery from the recession of 1990, placing us back on the growth curve. Present day debt growth curves are very steep.

This book uses the idea of compound growth to set the time frame in which the profit system will self destruct. Even if we deliberately increase governmental debt hoping to save the profit system we will fail. Compound growth becomes so rapid that our needed debt increase can not keep up. If this book falls short and fails to give you a feel for compound growth, perhaps you can find some person with knowledge of high school algebra to aid your understanding. (That person might appreciate your knowledge about system law in a profit system.)

In summary, no physical growth, not even intentional governmental debt, can increase at a positive rate of compound growth. To avoid permanent depression, a profit system must maintain a debt growth at some compound rate growth, and that is not possible. Changing the wording, our profit system which has worked both well and poorly for more than 200 years is doomed to self destruction.

The conclusion is unavoidable. You and I have laid a foundation of cause and effect economics knowledge based on systems law and the profit system process. That knowledge forces us to predict the future complete failure of our profit system, worldwide. It is important to note that as long as credit extension is enough to give a compound profit increase of buying power, the profit system will continue to operate. Not until credit is either pinched or becomes totally unable to increase at a mature compound rate will the profit system collapse in panic and stagnation. There is a little time, an indefinite amount, still left.

This book has not been written as advise on how to make a fortune by investments. This book is an early warning. The future is tumbling down on top of us! When failure occurs, it will happen very abruptly. You are very important to our future. Prior to the full collapse of our profit system, it is necessary for mankind to devise and transition to a nonprofit system of production and distribution. This conclusion can not be over emphasized. If we try to beat around the bush, deny reality, and try to keep the profit system, then our civilization will likely fall.

Chapter 3.
Profit System Ethics

We have been traveling very fast in our study of economics. The reason for the speed is that we have taken a short cut, and have not become tangled in unessential detail. For example, we have not spent pages on study of the stock exchange. Until now, stock has not even been mentioned. It was not necessary, as we developed a process explanation of the profit system. Also, in the first two chapters, little was said about morality. We only looked at the economic system as a process, as an impersonal machine, that we observed to see if it would work or not. The effect that use of the profit system has had on people's behavior and ethics is also very important to our quality of life.

As we now shift into consideration of profit system ethics, we should acknowledge the high living standard and also the vast destructiveness of profit system use so far. We want to see what use of the profit system has done for people and to people. We will not be alone as we look upon waste and exploitation of natural resources, and upon the crushing of people that has taken place. A difficult task will be tried. We will try to seperate human ethics from ethics of an economics system.

You may say that an economic system can not be unethical any more than an earthquake is, a hurricane or tornado is. The idea will be presented that an economic system can greatly influence the way people treat each other. If it strongly influences us into jungle law life, then the economic system is unethical.

There is an important factor as this book takes up the subject of ethics. Ethics, or morality, is highly subjective. My opinion that something is immoral might be disagreed with by some one else, and maybe by nearly every one else. The reverse is of course true. Other people might think something is immoral and my opinion would be that it was entirely ethical.

All my life there have been statements made around me that people are naturally cruel, pitiless, and vicious, acting kindly only because other people "civilized" them. There is inherent contradiction in these statements. Where do the "civilized" people come from to train the others into becoming civilized?

My opinion is that people are kind and helpful with each other in spite of being forced to live by jungle law much of the time. My opinion is that basic human nature is not cruel. My belief is that people are not "rotten to the core", but at the core are deeply considerate of other people's well being.

Such a sweeping opinion asks for support that goes beyond mere statement. First, we still exist. If we were far more vicious than kind, we long ago would have destroyed all of what we call mankind. Our continued existence is self-evident proof that people are not solely jungle law creatures but actually overcome jungle law to a remarkable degree. We may look at the often cruel way people behave and mistakenly think it is caused by human nature. Instead, that behavior could be chiefly the result of the economic system we use.

For one hour each week, little boys and girls go to Sunday school where they are taught, "Love Thy Neighbor." For the rest of the week those children are taught "be hard headed business people" able to survive in the economic struggle. With this imbalance of time spent in children's training, how do we explain the behavior of people during a disaster? The first law of life is survival, yet time after time during disaster, big or small, people have risked their lives to save the lives of other people.

You may feel that we are too easily passing out halos to all of mankind. Maybe we should continue the subject a bit further. People live in what might be termed a life boat situation, with some boats small, some large, and some people swimming. If you are in a small boat, your survival is in greater risk than if you are in a big boat. Yet people in small boats often try to help those who have no boat. This time, this is not just my opinion. There is history to look at. During the sinking of ships at sea, people safe (?) in life boats often pick swimmers out of the water to an extent which threatens to sink the life boat. I feel that these people who help others in need are demonstrating basic human nature.

History also tells us that some people brutally force their way onto life boats, drink more than their share of rationed water, eat more than their share of scarce food, and reject swimmers even when there is room on the boat. These people seem to contradict any truth in the claim that basic human nature is benevolent. If the benevolence is basic, then where does the brutal self-serving come from?

If you will remember that the following interpretation is opinion, let's think about the situation faced by people in a life boat that is so full it is in danger of sinking. From that time, no more swimmers can be picked up. All people in the boat, regardless of their benevolence, must subsequently abandon all swimmers. Now we have basic human nature plus situational necessity. The situation starts a behavioral change.

When a rescuing steamship, (a bigger life boat), finds the small life boat, all the people from the small boat go aboard the steamer. Rescued benevolent people, safer now, begin to forget that swimmers are still in the sea. Some people, sufficiently insecure and frightened in early childhood, would likely have their fears and insecurity exaggerated by life's endless life boat situation. This could bring a resolve to never be a swimmer, and to grab ever bigger life boats, taking them away from other people, by force when necessary. Perhaps years later these people each have a very large ship of their own, armed with machine guns to keep swimmers and small life boats at a distance. Perhaps they stand on their foredeck, look out at the swimmers and say, "Why don't you silly people get yourselves life boats?"

On the sea, this is the pattern in which people may change from deep consideration to almost total disregard of other people's welfare. If the life boat situation is a true analogy to life in our economic system, then we can expect an interaction between people's behavior and the pattern of economics.

Looking at profit system ethics is somewhat like eating a bunch of grapes. We can start with nearly any grape on the outside of the bunch. Based on knowledge from Chapter 2, we will start with competition and it's effect on people.

You possibly were surprised, reading Chapter 2, to see the statement that competition could be intense between businesses that are not in the same kind of business. The automobile industry is in competition with the clothing industry. Each automobile dealership is in competition with each clothing store. Each business is trying to retrieve investment and take profit out of the total buying power pool. If buying power is plentiful, both types of business, automobile and clothing, tend to enjoy success. If buying power is increasing too slowly to meet profit demand, then people may have too little money for a major purchase like a new car, but have enough money to buy clothing. Clothing businesses then would tend to absorb profit from the buying power pool, getting that profit by taking money invested by automobile businesses. Continued long enough, this can be serious enough to cause automobile business failures.

You ask, "What does this unintentional competition have to do with ethics? People in the clothing business are not even aware that the clothing business profit is causing automobile business failures. How can clothing business people be blamed for that ?" That is the point. Clothing business people can not be blamed for this unaware and unintentional harm to the automobile business owner and his employees. The economic procedures cause the harm. Far out? People's behavior did not even need to be changed for harm to be done.

Now we face the question of whether or not a process in an economic system can be immoral, or if instead, something can be immoral only if people are deliberately causing it. It is my feeling that the result is what counts, whether people or an economic process creates the result.

The profit process has historically been one that allowed vast numbers of people to establish businesses during times when money increase was sufficient to make new businesses possible. Maybe the people were able to make their businesses continue to prosper for years by doing long hours of work and hiring help who contributed in the effort to make the businesses thrive. Then came the pinch when all these increasing numbers of thriving business could not find enough new money increase to make the profit system work. By an economic system process, unknown and unintended by people, a great percentage of the formerly thriving businesses were forced into failure. All the thinking, the enthusiasm, the investment of money, and years of effort were wiped out merely because money increase fell behind profit system demand. This is the historical pattern. Across the nation during deep depression, the unlucky businesses number in the thousands, and there are millions of employees who lose their jobs. I feel that the system is immoral.

A prime reason for the long time use of the profit system is the profit motive. This is both a blessing and a curse. It has often been said that the thirst for profit furnishes the driving power causing people to establish and build the businesses which give the production and distribution so essential to society. However, the drive for profit also causes many business owners to do everything legally possible to drive some other business out of existence. This competition is intentional, most often between business of like kind. This business competition is sometimes very cutthroat, often intense, and never non existent.

On the surface, this appears to be cruelty by people, not economic system fault. The business person who uses crushing methods on his way to wealth may be the product of childhood insecurities so great that he has to dominate to compensate for them.

Although there are obvious examples of people reaching for wealth by stepping all over other people, most people, including a high percentage of the wealthy, are kind hearted and would avoid taking unfair advantage of other people. However, even highly numerous benevolent people may learn to disregard the existence of much poorer people. Learned disregard may reinforce the behavior of people who are unmerciful in working their way upward. I am implying that much of the widespread, sometimes deep, lack of concern for other people today is the group reaction of living all our lives in the jungle law profit sytem.

It does not seem likely that people are so basically hostile to each other that they deliberately devised jungle law business. More likely, knowing no better way of life, people of ancient times adopted a dog-eat-dog jungle law life which continued as the profit system. A danger to mankind is that we recognize and condemn cut-throat competiton as jungle law but fail to see our responsibility when we condone mutual destruction of unlike businesses during days of deficient money increase. "Where does human kindliness stop, taken over by the daily sub-surface ruthlessness demanded by profit system survival?"

The effects of business competition by nations will be considered later in this chapter. Also to be considered later are the exaggerated effects of severe depressions suffered by the profit system.

New business concerns are constantly being started. A large percent succeed. Some fail early from many causes, such as poor management. Most failures result from unintentional elimination during periods of insufficient buying power increase. Bigger businesses tend to survive best, running out of reserves less quickly. Survivors tend to grow and exlude their competition when buying power again increases enough to give prosperity. Historically, bigger business has taken over an ever increasing percentage of the nation's total business activity. A force seems to work towards existence of fewer businesses, with the surviving businesses growing to giant size, and even monopoly.

Large sized business has been a great benefit to the general population in one important way. About a dozen years before our American Revolution, large business enabled the start of the industrial revolution. Without great wealth accumulated by merchants and land owners before the start of the industrial revolution, that revolution could not have occured so easily. Wealth was necessary to build factories and machines which brought mechanized production to replace manual production.

The industrial revolution enabled businesses to grow larger with ever greater speed. What a break for wealthy people. Investing wealth brought increasing wealth, ever more rapidly. What a break for the general population. The living standard rose as a result of the productivity of machines. More, better, and less expensive products generally resulted. The general living standard no longer was limited by muscle power and the dexterity of hands.

In coming pages, some items of United States history will be skimmed for specific situations of people's behavior in our economic system. Very few examples will be picked from the situations that abound in history. While using your cookie jar insight, also observe the constant existence of jungle law which pressured both business people and workers to ignore their conscience.

In the United States, the first transcontinental railroad would not have been possible if businesses all were too small. Big business has certainly served a useful purpose. It has also brought great problems.

Thirty one years before our Civil War, Robert Stevens invented the "T" rail, greatly improving railroad capability. During the next twenty years, the number of railroad companies increased to a few hundred. As the number of railroad companies grew, so did the size of some of them. One reason was that some railroads bought competing railroads. Related to that was the power of large companies to eliminate small companies. Seldom was the reverse true, with small companies bumping large companies out of the way. Rapidly, big companies began to eliminate small ones. Big ones then grew bigger, and the number of railroad companies decreased.

An aid to the growth of railroad companies was the governmental grant of land to companies for cross continent right-of-way. Grants were not given to tiny companies. Only companies big enough to extend track long distances received the gifts of land. This favored big companies, which grew bigger. Tiny companies tended to disappear entirely.

This granting of land was heavy during the 1850's following the 1849 beginning of the gold rush to California. The land grants were planned to increase rail mileage rapidly to tie our nation together. In 1869, railroads formed a transportation base for expansion from sea to shining sea.

We will cover only a few of many adverse factors that accompanied the great advantages from railroad transportation.

The legend of the James brothers, Jesse and Frank, tells us that land grants to the rialroads sometimes resulted in some very pushy land acquisition. Any existing farm family in the way of railroad right-of-way was subject to being shoved out of the way. The retreat of the American Indians was made permanent by the advance of the Iron Horse. People from the eastern part of our country no longer were limited to wagon trains as a means of moving west. The migrating settlers held the profit system view that land was to be held in private ownership. This was totally different from the American Indian belief that the land belonged to the Great Spirit, with people using that land only temporarily. With the aid of the moneymaking fast-advancing Iron Horse, communal land passed to private ownership. The owners of the railroads and the other new owners of land did not seem to feel guilty.

Among the problems scattered along the railroad tracks was that of safety for the railroad workers. Pre Civil War insurance companies would not insure railroad crews. The life was too dangerous. For example, before development of automatic couplers between cars, there was many a brakeman disasterously caught betwen cars during train hook up.

Freight rates and passenger rates were not set by the customers. How could the customer argue rates with the owner of a railroad when that railroad was the only one near? Rates were arbitrary, unreasonable, and even different to favor one shipper over another.

Almost like a law of nature, railroad companies became fewer and bigger. Soon after the Civil War, the surviving railroads became enormous systems. The owners controlled huge empires, sometimes created by better service, sometimes build with mergers, and sometimes the result of very disreputable methods of competition. During this growth, the railroad owners seemed to increasingly disregard the welfare of the general population.

Full circle was acheived. Formation of big business, such as railroading, benefited the public by increasing the standard of living. Formation of giant business also created a class of people so wealthy they had more money and power than our national government. When big business got big enough, it was prone to act as if the population existed for the benefit of big business.

Speaking again about railroading, by 1870 the general population's anger against big railroad behavior brought a clamor for national government legislation attempting to control railroads. The interstate nature of railroading had made the local laws of states fairly ineffective. Perhaps the national government would have been ineffective also, given the wealth and power of big railroad companies. In 1873, there was a financial panic, a small depression. Railroad companies were hard hit. During a time when railroad companies were weakest and the nation was scared about its economic future, some national legislation was passed putting a rein on railroads. It is possible that our country barely escaped complete loss of democracy, submerged by railroad power, but saved by depression.

There is a side point for us to think about, here. We can make use of cookie jar law to understand the probable cause of the 1873 panic. The entire national economy was still small at the time. Total money in the system was not large, although money increase coming from the 1849 gold rush had given prosperity. The immense profit taken by huge railroad companies likely was enough to drain the money supply, bringing the panic.

Because they could not get insurance, pre Civil War railroad workers formed labor unions, some of the earliest in the country. The goal of the unions was group financial assistance to individual workers in event of injury, or assistance to the families of workers who died in work accidents. Railroad companies seldom gave this assistance.

Failure of early day railroads to give financial assistance when railroad crewmen were hurt or killed is part of a profit system axiom. That which is good for a business may be bad for the workers. That which is good for the workers may harm the business.

Let's return to pre American Civil War time, and talk about railroads as an example of all business of the time. You may feel that an 1850 railroad business is not a good enough example for us to make general statements about profit system ethics. The time, the 1850's, was chosen to predate labor union and legislative efforts to control wages and work conditions. You can not tell the nature of a dog that is muzzled and on a leash. The essentially unfettered big business railroads look to me like a good example to show basic ethics of a profit system.

Greatly improving safety for railroad crews in 1850, for example, would have been both difficult and costly for railroad companies. Increased safety involving equipment improvements would generally depend upon invention and better design. Better safety design took time, inspiration, and effort. Changing to better equipment would likely require outlay of much money, especially if outmoded equipment had to be scrapped. The owners might have strongly wished to make their train crews safe, but the cost could have been loss of profit and jeopardized business survival.

If railroad owners had compensated workmen for accidents and families in case of workmen deaths, the expense would have been large. The extent of danger to workmen was shown by refusal of coverage by insurance companies. Perhaps railroad owners wished that they were able to pay direct compensation for accidents, but were afraid of the high cost.

The combined cost of safer equipment and cost of accident compensation would likely have endangered business survival of small railroads. Increased safety and direct workmen's compensation was not paid for by big companies with ability to pay. Evidence of ability is the huge wealth that some owners reaped from the railroad business.

Perhaps greed was the driving force behind the accumulation of great wealth at the expense of railroad worker safety. Maybe there was a class system with a wide gap between railroad worker and railroad owner. It could be that the owners even felt haughty disdain for mere employees.

At the risk of over excusing greed and arrogance of wealth, I wish to lay much blame on the nature of our economic system. Remember the story of the person who stood on the foredeck of a large ship? Machine guns were mounted to keep small life boats and swimmers at a distance. No ship is ever big enough to dispel some people's fear of becoming merely a swimmer. No amount of wealth is enough to stop the scramble for ever greater wealth. My implication is that the profit system forces a callous and uncaring behavior towards people, maybe contrary to the consideration actually felt by business owners.

The 1850's railroad workman was expected to offer hard labor for long hours under dangerous and unhealthy conditions. The business owners also had to work long hours to succeed, and they risked their investment. However, if they started to fail, they could sell, or recover a portion of their investment. The workmen risked their very lives, making them possible human sacrifices to success of someone else's business.

There were a multitude of social imbalances in 1850's railroading. There was a big difference between the owner's income and any workman's take-home pay. There was a disparity of bargaining power when a business owner and a workman talked about wages or working conditions. An individual workman asking for a pay raise found that he was facing a big railroad that simply could fire him just for requesting a pay raise. Jungle law.

The workmen knew that the owners lived in large houses, often set on huge tracts of land. There were costly social events, and the owners lived remote and aloof from the workmen's social life. Because the owner's standard of living was so obviously greater than that of the workmen, the workmen could hardly avoid being quite resentful. The railroad owners could hardly be unaware of the resentment. Since the cause never went away, the resentment never went away either. Thus each of the two groups, the business owners and the workers, lived with varying degrees of hatred for the other group. They needed each other, and they hated each other, continuously.

It appears that the profit system creates group hatred. This is a large and important part of profit system ethics. The profit system tends to set the worker group and the business owners against each other.

In spite of the basic enmity between wealthy business owners and the "working class", the workers in the United States did not launch the economic revolution predicted by mid 1800 writers such as Karl Marx. Mutual antagonism created by use of the profit system remained in check for a variety of reasons.

Business owners and workers have at least one common goal. Both groups want success for the particular business they are in. Workmen want their job source to flourish. Business owners have to have workers. This mutual need forms the only strong basis for cooperation between owners and workers. The truce is never untroubled, but it has tended to avert revolution.

It seems that a great many workmen, at least in each new generation, believe they might someday get their own business and become rich. A few do succeed. Most merely hope. The large number who hope also condone the existence of the large difference between the workman's income and social status and that of the owners of big business.

Workers may have been resigned to a massive process which seemed too large for individuals to change. Alex de Toqueville wrote about something being "Endured so long as it seemed beyond redress." As a result, forced change was not tried. However, a possibly stronger reason was widespread basic faith in the American way of life. As long as workmen could find employment in jobs paying for even a slow increase in living standard, there was a margin of safety from revolution.

In our nation, unlike places such as Europe, we had open land onto which people could move. In the mid 1800's, there was a vast area of sparcely populated land which could be settled by anyone disgruntled with treatment by big business in the east. This open frontier relieved a great amount of animosity and established the optimistic view of life which dominated the United States.

A very strong factor decreasing economic unrest was the existence of democracy here. Our type of government softened some of the harsher inequities of profit system life. An example is the passage of laws aiding coal mine company town residents. There was a time period during which coal mines became big business. Many coal mine companies built entire small towns on company owned land where coal was abundant. Low paid mine workers often received company issued certificates instead of U.S. money for their work. These certificates were popularly called scrip, and could be spent no where except in the company store or to pay rent for a company owned house. Think of the song "Sixteen Tons" sung by Tennessee Ernie Ford, and the phrase, "I owe my soul to the company store." You see the pattern of life for most coal mine workers of those days.

Without legal currency to spend elsewhere, the coal miner found that he and his family were trapped in the company town. Laws were passed to force coal mine companies to pay miners in legal tender money instead of company scrip.

Even if it did not become easy, it became much more possible for the miner to move away.

Large sized business was put on a leash and muzzled to a degree by passage of laws as the years went by. This book is not a history about the great number of laws passed trying to limit the power of huge business. A bare minimum of history is considered to carry the idea that profit system businesses tended to act in a very greedy and inconsiderate way towards working people and consumers.

While American faith in democracy stopped economic revolution in the United States, some other areas of the world were not so lucky. In 1917, economic and political revolution did occur in Russia and the surrounding area. Russia was under Czarist dictatorship. The revolution appears to have grown out of very severe political repression teamed with widespread abject poverty alongside of great wealth.

Our democratic government has been very important in saving us from revolution. Yet, when we speak of democracy in our country, we are very apt to talk as though our private enterprise profit system is democracy, itself. Such a thought is an error. Private enterprise profit businesses are not democracy. Democracy is our political structure, not our economic system.

Democracy is, "We, the people." We get together to agree on laws by which we cooperate. We also choose representatives to make laws by which we can cooperate. We form a constitution which limits the laws that our representatives may make for us. The same constitution instructs and limits the people who administer our laws. The constitution places the military service, which is a dictatorship, under control by our elected representatives. We cautiously modify our laws and constitution to fit changing conditions and increased wisdom.

As we work towards rule by law, we people retain supremacy over it all. There is slippage in how effective we are in insisting that our representative government stays aware of people's supremacy over government.

With everything we do, our ultimate not-quite reachable goal is elimination of jungle law. Democracy is the route.

It is very easy to be aware of dictatorship whenever it appears. Dictatorship is, "I" and "Me". Dictators do say say you, also. They say, "I want you to do what I say, and if you don't I will force you, using violence if necessary." Dictators tell the military what to do, and use the military to enforce the will of the dictators. In a full dictatorship, everthing which is not ordered is forbidden.

Private enterprise for profit is almost always a mass of individual dictatorships. It camouflages under the guise of individual freedom, a goal of democracy.

In the tiniest size of profit system business, one person performs a service, or produces or buys to sell at a profit. This tiniest private enterpise is not a dictatorship. However, the first time that a person hires another and tells that person what to do, the business becomes a dictatorship. Neither is it truly private enterprise any longer, but group enterprise. The name, private enterprise, is a misnomer, but we will still use it for two reasons. We want to use the long established name so people will understand what we refer to. Also, public enterprise would be governmental activity, or other activity for the benefit of the people.

In so called private enterprise where one or more people work under the control of a person or company, there is a boss. Where there is a boss, there is dictatorship.

Amongst the writings of Charles Dickens, there was a Christmas time story about a boss. Scrooge owned a business, a tiny one. Scrooge squeezed the last possible bit of effort from an employee, but paid wages on which the employee's family could hardly subsist. Charles Dickens ascribed this state of affairs to the bitter greed of Mr. Scrooge. A change of heart brought lavish Christmas aid to the employee's family, higher pay promised, and beginnings of happiness for Scrooge as he became less greedy.

In spite of my great respect for Mr. Dickens' insight into the tyranny of profit system business, I feel he overlooked the trap that Mr. Scrooge was in. Survival of a business tends to mandate that a business owner boss maximize the output of an employee while minimizing the pay. Appearance of greed may exist while greed may not be felt. However, years of being a Scrooge from necessity may become such a habit that this behavior can not be easily discarded. This is the pattern of profit system ethics. Profit system procedures are dictatorial, and they teach the habits of dictatorship.

Employees are continuously forced into acceptance of dictatorship in the work day world. At home, democracy may prevail. On the way to or from work, an employee may pass within an environment that is mainly democracy. At work, the employee does what the business owner commands. Regardless of the softness of voice, politeness and esteem shown by the wording, the commands are those of dictatorship.

If you were a tourist in Europe, perhaps in France, you could be asked what the Unites States is. If you were a typical tourist, you would likely respond by claiming that the United States is a democracy. But thinking back only one paragraph, we know that dictatorship exists thoughout all of the business world of the United States. The number of people involved in the dictatorial business part of our nation far outnumbers those engaged in our representative governmental democracy. The time spent under economic dictatorship far exceeds time selecting people to represent us in our political democracy. As a nation, we are a contradiction, a mix of political democracy and economic dictatorship.

In school, students are told about democracy's heroes, such well known people as Washington, Franklin, Jefferson, and many thousand lesser known people who also worked and fought for democracy. After dilligent effort, the students know many names of democracy's heroes. After graduation from school and entry into the work force, former students probably seldom recall democracy's heroes. The work force is too busy making a living in an economic dictatorship.

Why is this part defeat of democracy tolerated? Maybe it is because most of our ancestors allowed it, so we have inherited their tolerance for daily dictatorship. Maybe it is because we have not contrived a non-dictatorial method of producing and distributing. Maybe our fairly high living standard blinds us, makes us complacent. Also, economic dictatorship is not unified, but is made up of many thousands of little businesses and a few thousand big businesses. We can easily fail to recognize these separated groups as a national dictatorship. Yet, along with complacency, there is a sub-surface opposition to the daily tyranny, often appearing as wry humor about the worker and the boss.

Three hundred and sixty five days a year we go about our business of production and distribution, using private enterprise groups, each dictatorial from top to bottom. These exist alongside of our governmental democracy which makes laws somewhat limiting the extent of dictatorial economic power.

Labor unions have also helped to hold private enterprise powers in check. Labor unions have at times become nearly powerful enough to balance the power of big business. Without this strong assistance from unions, it is likely that government could not alone have placed limitations on private enterprise. Economic dictatorships might have joind hands sufficiently to suppress our political democracy into extinction.

The members of unions once may have thought that if their entire membership refused to work, the union's demands would be conceded by business. This seemed a peaceful method. In spite of large numbers of people in a union, businesses were often able to replace all union members with new employees. This meant defeat for the unions, and sudden unemployment. When mass refusal to work was not effective, picketing job locations and harassment of the replacement employees was tried. This step led towards violence.

Bigger businesses that could afford to do so hired armed guards to protect new employees and business property. In protracted labor strikes, the business affected had its survival threatened. The union members and their families grew hungry and angry. Heavy sabotage of business property has occured. Deaths have widely been part of the industrial warfare.

There is very little democracy existing in an intense labor dispute, with both sides suffering. The general public, the consumer, suffers with the two battling factions. This three way suffering is a part of profit system ethics.

Labor unions tended to be controlled by the votes of union membership. This injected some democracy into our economic system where there was otherwise only dictatorship. The degree of democracy depended upon the relative strength of a union and a business, with a power struggle occuring most of the time. Also, some union officials have become bosses of the union, taking so much control that the rank-and-file members became insignificant. Thus, these members escaped from the power of the big business owner only to be entrapped into obeying a union boss in order to have union unity. Profit system ethics again damaged the individual.

Occasionally, business owners used bribes to fight unions. Union representatives sent to bargain with business owners sometimes were induced to betray the union. When bribes were accepted, the economic demcoracy represented by unions has been defeated.

Corruption of the kind exemplified by offering and taking bribes is contagious. Sometimes government officials, not union officials, are the bribe takers. Sometimes this type of corruption is glaringly obvious. Some may take place unknown by any one except those closest involved. Much takes place with many people slightly or fully aware. The profit system process seems to have an abundance of unethical and marginally ethical action. It swirls and eddies around people as they earn a living. Some people support, some condone, and some condemn this basic jungle law. Even people who condemn may feel pressure to cheat in order to survive amongst other cheaters.

People endlessly subjected to life

in an environment of tolerated corruption become immune to objecting. People carry home their feelings of acceptance of unethical activities, infecting their families. If most people opposed the jungle law environment of earning a living, there would be change. Since no change happens, it would appear that most either support or condone the process of the big and powerful eating the small and weaker. The corrosive effect of condonement over a long period of time shows when you hear, "Why shouldn't I? Everyone is doing it." It is amazing that people even partly reject the habits of corruption, economic treachery, and other patterns of jungle law that we are exposed to so frequently by our economic system. Profit system ethics, "anything for a dollar," colors our national character with a strong stain.

Before we leave industrial conflict behind, let us emphasize an idea touched on once before. The idea: using industrial conflict, people try to better their personal financial condition. The profit process very impersonally cancels people's efforts. Apply cookie jar law to the union and industry wage increase pattern. The workers ask for higher pay. Industry grants higher pay, knowing that goods and services will subsequently be sold at a higher price to consumers. But workers are the main consumers. The higher pay is cancelled by higher cost of living. The entire pattern repeats. Prices go one way, which is up. Once initiated, the cause and effect chain will occur almost with certainty.

In the wage-price upward spiral lies

two lessons, both based on the machine-like reaction of the profit system to industrial conflict. The first lesson is that the system places both workers and businesses into inflation, the very situation they had tried to escape. Conflict repeats endlessly. The profit system is endlessly immoral.

The second lesson is that inflation decreases effective money, hastening depression and much suffering. Ironically, the profit system has within itself a force which tends to hasten its self destruction.

The conflict which arises from confrontations between labor unions and business also arises between nations. Use of the profit system has had a strong effect on the relationship between nations. Let's very briefly consider bits of history from the early relationship between England, colonial New England, and a little later, the newly formed United States.

The industrial revolution, bringing use of power machinery and factories, only shortly predated the American Revolution. England quickly became the manufacturing center of the world. First, easily understandable by use of system law, England's manufacturing and merchant businesses could not sell all of their produce inside their "home market," the island of England. England was a cohesive group of many businesses, plus its population, but the nation acted like a single business concern, selling to foreign markets. Business activities were often reinforced by military dominance.

Colonial New England was looked upon as a source of raw materials to be converted by England's factories and sold to consumers in New England. Exploitation of the colonial market was intentional. King George collected taxes from the colonies, and England's commercial people collected profits.

As England drained buying power from Colonial New England, the Colonies suffered. To maintain English dominance, the Colonies were politically restricted from making steel and other products which competed with English production. The Colonies revolted. Conclusion: profit system pressures tend to cause war.

Prohibition of manufacturing in New England could not be fully enforced, so some factory type industry did begin before the Revolutionary War. Start of the War freed America's fledgling industry from England's restrictions. Also, the need for war materials made demands which brought industrial growth. The war gave us both political freedom from England and incentive to strengthen our industry.

After the Revolutionary War was won and the United States was established, it kept the political freedom. Newly growing industry in our country did not fare so well. The long established factories in England were far superior to our factories. Our new nation was treated to a heavy dose of profit system competition on a national scale. The price of England's production was below the price of American production. American factories were devastated by the unequal competition. For nearly 30 years, the new United States of America remained under economic domination by England. England's government helped sustain the imbalance by forbidding English exportation of factory machines and designs.

Until 1812, England's economic power seems to have restricted our industry more strongly than their pre-war political power did. England's industrial and commercial businesses, each an economic dictatorship, almost cancelled the benefits of our political democracy. In the half dozen years before 1812, American shippping was severely restricted by both France and England, at war with each other. Foreign trade was the source of goods not yet produced in America. The restriction of American shipping resulted in hardship to United States consumers and commercial people. Our merchant ships, unlike our factories, were amongst the best in the world. England was not allowing free use of our merchant ships, especially blocking trade with France. When English war ships stopped American merchant ships at sea, kidnapping American sailors to man English war ships, the United States declared war on England.

Although the trigger for war may have been the kidnapping of American seamen, most of the pressures leading to the War of 1812 were commercial and financial. The very young United States was both the newest and the oldest democracy. Power of the democracy was in the people, but as individuals, the commercial and business people held the most power. Looking into our history of the time, it appears that the main reason for declaration of war against England was financial.

When the United States declared war in 1812, the avowed purpose was to break free of the very hampering restrictions placed on trade between the United States and foreign countries. There seems to be much evidence that England was acting like a big military bully, so much so that the United States was justified in a war of self defense. Yet an important factor is that someone, probably England, used national military force to win in the struggle for foreign markets. Then, and ever since, we have seen nations use military force to obtain or keep foreign markets, or to protect their home markets. This is profit system ethics on a national scale.

All of the conditions that occur with competition between businesses within a nation apply to the competition between nations. Really, we can drop the words "between nations" because the competition is mostly between businesses in one country all competing with each other and with all businesses in all other countries. Remember, too, that each kind of business is competing with businesses of all other kinds. Each business is trying to recover its investment plus profit from the international money pool. The world encloses all business inside of one system just as effectively as the island did in our multi business trade example in Chapter 2. Military war to establish prosperity by trade dominance is an asinine effort.

The struggle for foreign markets has

resulted, and can still result, in wars. Prior to World War II, Adolf Hitler rose to power in Germany when he stirred that nation to rebel against economic restrictions placed on it at the end of World War I. If we concentrate all of the goals that Hitler had, they amount to making Germans the master of the economies of all other nations. Germany was militarily going to force all other nations into becoming foreign markets. As each nation was conquered, its population was to become near slaves, producing goods for sale. It was expected that this would result in great profit for the master nation. Hitler and his Nazis had no idea that slaves are a very poor market. Had Hitler been successful in enslaving the world, the entire economy would have collapsed because you can't take more cookies out of a jar than there are in it. Slaves do not have many cookies.

Except when undeniably done for self defense, war is probably the ultimate immorality, the tops in unethical behavior. Economic chaos is close behind. You will have to be the judge as to whether Hitler was the villain, or whether profit system goals carried to extreme shared equal or greater blame.

During World War II, war at last became capable of destroying all civilization, if not all of mankind. The atomic bomb developed during war was made more powerful after the war, getting its name changed to nuclear bomb. Rocket powered missiles became capable of inter continental range, carrying the nuclear warheads. The nations having these missiles and nuclear bombs became capable of complete destruction of another nation half way around the world. From orbiting satellite stations, observation of nuclear armed missile lauches became possible, allowing enough warning to enable retaliatory launches from the nation under attack. Thus, missiles traveling in opposite directions gave nations both the ability to destroy a nation half way around the world and the assurance that the attacking nation would also be destroyed by retaliatory missiles. This condition was aptly named "mutually assured destruction". Mad.

Ironic humor said that an atomic bomb attack could ruin a person's entire day. War has long been the most destructive activity engaged in by mankind. It wastes people and things, and falls fartherest short of being common sense. Even if war on a nuclear scale fails to develop, the sustained arming of nations to nuclear war capability is a massive drain on economies.

Each and ever economist, such as you if you are a father or mother with a family, is interested in stopping the nonsense economics of war. Each of you humanitarians is interested in stopping the nonsense slaughter and maiming. My opinion is that there is a nearly unsurmountable obstacle to stopping war if you wait until it starts, or if heavy threat of war exists. To object at that time will only get you labelled unpatriotic, and you will be ignored, or shot. We actually owe our ultimate "patriotism" to mankind. If mankind is ever going to irradicate war before it irradicates us, the mass of mankind must act against war during time of peace. That action must be to find and remove causes of war.

Economic causes are not the only causes of war, but economic causes may be possible to control. The profit system goads business people into treating each other in a restrained warlike manner, with the restraints ready to disappear at times. If economic conditions are tough in the home market, we tend to go farther afield into foreign markets, searching for profit. If we have a proven high capability for production that needs to be sold, we can get nearly belligerant if some other nation refuses to be our "foreign market". If that hoped for foreign market is a nation with a high capability for production that needs to be sold to us, we face profit system ethics on an international scale.

A useful quality of money is it gives some freedom of choice. If the money pool is full enough to allow spending other than for mere subsistence, the consumer may choose to buy an automobile. The car chosen may be foreign made. Perhaps the chosen car was manufactured in a nation where the base pay for labor is one fourth the rate in our home nation. (These exaggerated rates are for illustration only.) Because of low labor costs, the chosen foreign made car can be purchased for perhaps half the price charged for a comparable car manufactured in one's home nation. If this should become a pattern for many home nation consumers, sizeable amounts of money flows from the home nation and into the foreign nation.

You know the secondary result. The home automobile maker begins to suffer financially. One way to compensate is for the home nation car maker to make the car cheaper, not only in price, but in cost by lowering the quality. You guess that the next result is that home nation consumers continue to buy the foreign made auto because foreign makers used their profit to improve their product -- still at a low price. My conclusion is that your guess would be correct, and that home nation auto makers may discharge many of their employees to cut down on expenses. My question next is how can unemployed employees buy any automobiles, home or foreign?

Maybe the highly praised "invisible hand" of the immensely praised "free market" would bring market adjustments a year or a few downstream. This "home market"/"foreign market" situation involves millions of people who suffer disruptions to their livelihood. Of course you know that this story is an analogy to the United States and Japan at the start of the year 1992. You of course have looked at this situation from the viewpoint of system law. You probably shudder a bit, thinking that this innocent profit system competition on an international basis could become ugly and bring out use of force.

In our home market, or in international "trade", the flow of money from consumers is like a vote. Money gives choice. As you read towards the last chapter of this book, remember the idea that our medium of exchange, money in this case, gives people a daily vote to control what is manufactured and who makes it. Also, look back to the quotation marks around the word trade. True trade involves just what you think it does: exchange of useful items for some one else's useful items. Trade is not a "for profit" transaction, even if one party involved gets more out of the exchange than the other does. The word "trade" has been used so much for any financial transaction that true meaning is made obscure. We have lost a word that was once quite specific, and can now use it in only a general way. "Balance of trade" and "trade deficit" are not appropriate words for the flow of money from the pockets of consumers into foreign pockets. Buying a foreign car is a profit process subject to system law.

As money flows and surges like a tide from the people of one nation to the people of another nation, the system nature of the profit process is exhibited quite openly. It is beyond my understanding that people remain unaware of the system law explanation of all profit processes as they observe the foreign market activity. People talk and write, getting very near to the truth, yet fall short.

As the year of 1991 closed, recession (a denial word for beginning depression) afflicted the United States. Money had flowed out of the U. S. money pool, creating a national decrease of money in a portion of a system which demands a money increase. The money flow had been into Japan, satisfying Japan's regional profit system demand for a money increase. People enmass in the United States understood that the outflow of money was quickly bringing recession. People enmass in the United States failed to take the extra step in understanding that both Japan and the United States are tied together, irrevocably, in a world profit system that must respond to system law.

During the year of 1991, debt increase (money increase) was failing to keep up with the profit demand of the world profit system. If debt increase had been adequate, then both Japan and the United States would have been enjoying increasing prosperity.

The year of 1991 has placed the profit system just about one year too far along the time coordinate of compound profit growth. Look back at the end of Chapter 2 where sample graphs show money increase demanded by compound profit rate growth. Every curve there enters a time period when the curve becomes extremely steep. Locking us into mathematical language, there are points in time for each curve when the yearly increase increment is beyond the ability of people to increase physical debt fast enough.

Please refrain from wasting time trying to determine which percentage curve applies today. We are on some curve where we are falling farther and farther behind the world profit demand. The profit system is getting ready to hit mankind with one of the greatest problems ever to face civilization. Grave danger awaits us when the profit system reaches the time when we can no longer contrive to increase debt sufficiently fast to sustain the demand for profit at a compound rate.

In a profit system, money (debt) flow generally starts with the consumer going into debt to buy something from the business people who slowly accumulate more and more of this money. Observation of financial history confirms that successful business owners reinvest, or capatilize, their profit. This results in ever faster aquisition of profit during an ample money pool. History confirms that businesses doing a major part of the successful business become ever larger, enabling them to take an ever greater portion of business. We need not be surprised that money does not follow a "trickle down" theory, but instead flows from consumers into a very heavy concentration of wealth in the hands of ever fewer individuals. Watch the tide.

In 1990, newspaper quoted statistics said that two percent of the population in the United States controlled 80 percent of the wealth. To get some idea of how much 80 percent of the wealth is, let's reverse the picture. That means that 98 percent of the population had to live on 20 percent of the total wealth. Since the 98 percent lived somewhat well on only 20 percent of the wealth, it gives you some idea of how much 80 percent of the wealth really is. This picture should be adjusted still more for probable accuracy.

We can not believe that 98 percent

of the population shared 20 percent 0f the wealth equally. It is probable that another 2 percent part of the 98 percent group controled 80 percent of the 20 percent of wealth. That would mean the second 2 percent group likely controlled 16 percent of the wealth. The remaining 96 percent of the population would have only 4 percent of the wealth to divide up. The latter picture is likely much more accurate than the one we first used for comparison. If 96 percent of the population lived somewhat well on only 4 percent of the wealth, you have a fairly good idea of how much 80 percent of the wealth is. That was shared by the top 2 percent of the population. Below is a table summarizing the preceding arithmetic.

Top 2 percent had 80 percent of wealth
Next 2 percent had 16 percent of wealth
Last 96 percent had 4 percent of wealth

The topmost income people within the 96 percent group are not amongst the rich, but they have some security in life. However, the bottommost income people within the 96 percent population group are the homeless, etc., people relying on charity from someone a bit less unfortunate. Some live by picking up aluminum cans to recycle, or by scrounging in dumpsters for anything useful, whether food or clothing.

Although a bit tedious, the above arithmetic gives a somewhat fair picture of wealth distribution in 1990 United States, and again now in 1998. The difference between the income of the top 2 percent and perhaps the bottom 2 percent

percent of the population is a staggering gap. The 2 percent of people at the bottom could not conceive what life is like for the 2 percent at the top. Neither is it likely that the 2 percent of the people who control 80 percent of the wealth can have any understanding of the bare existence life of the bottom 2 percent of people. The existence of these two extreme conditions was created by the profit system's never ceasing trend to concentrate wealth in ever fewer hands.

To me, it does not seem likely that our nation is in danger of a social uprising started by the poorest 5 percent of our population. The helplessly poor have been in that condition so long that they do not have hopes enough to start an uprising. However, any economic system that creates and maintains the disparity of wealth evident between the wealthy top 2 percent and perhaps the bottom 90 percent is causing a very unstable social condition. Rewording, the top 2 percent control 80 percent of the wealth. The bottom 90 percent control perhaps 4 percent of the wealth. Eighty percent of the wealth is divided by 2 percent of the population, while 4 percent of the wealth is divided amongst 90 percent of the population. That is a precariously top heavy social condition.

Any long sustained unemployment, such as the amount of unemployment at the start of 1992, will greatly lower the 4 percent of wealth controlled by probably 90 percent of the population. Democracy is not apt to be threatened by the 90 percent of the population which forms the backbone of democracy. However, if the anguish of unemployment is long continued, there will be obvious unrest, and reaction to that unrest could be greatly dangerous.

As impending profit system collapse begins to show, masses of people without knowledge of its cause might become quite tumultuous. During any self-destruct stage of the profit system, financial interests, internationally, may do anything in an effort to avoid the inevitable loss of status quo. They might combine the power of wealth with total lack of knowledge about the true cause of profit system self-destruct action. Misreading permanent collapse as temporary difficulty, the use of power of wealth to squelch unrest might seem all too logical. If the chaotic conditons of profit system collapse occur, then we risk the same danger as trying vainly to stop war once it has started. Maybe the hidden moral of this paragraph is that lack of knowledge in this situation is a stark invitation to disaster.

Perhaps 100 years ago when horses were very important, there was a saying that it was futile to beat a dead horse. It also is foolish. Futile implies meanness. Foolish implies unawareness about reality. The people who control the great wealth in the world would hardly be vengeful enough to beat a horse they knew was dead, or certain to die. Those same people could possibly be foolish enough to beat a horse they thought would still live. It might be quite a job to convince people, early enough to do good, that the profit system has in it the seed of certain self destruction. Lack of that knowledge is the seed to possible social explosion.

The Constitution of the United States makes the President of the United States responsible for maintaining an economy that is prosperous. We, the people, have chosen to use the profit system during all of our history so far. That system operates according to its simple basic design, and will continue its course according to that design as long as we continue to choose to use it. The president can not stop a glacier. The president can not stop the profit system from collapsing. He can affect the disparity of wealth, slowing or speeding the flow of money into the hands of those who control most of the wealth. The President can, as Ronald Reagan demonstrated, increase the national debt to many times more than it was. This type of vast debt increase temporarily satisfies the demand of the profit system for money increase, but it can not be sustained at the increase amount demanded by a soon to be 230 year old profit system. In spite of the responsibility that the Constitution says the President has, we should not hold him responsible for things beyond his control. We, the people, are responsible by our choice of a pattern of economics.

What should we think about the ethics of a group of people who maybe intentionally created prosperity? It was very easy for the wealthy investors during World War II to see that the vast growth of wartime national debt coincided with the vast profit which followed. It is just as easy for us to believe that those wealthy investors put their heads together after the war was over. "Look," they may have said in special gatherings, "prosperity followed the war time debt increase. Let us make use of this knowledge to continue prosperity for the entire United States, and also to plan our way to greater wealth. If we use our money power to influence governmental spending that we know about in advance, we should be able to cash in. The fastest pay off, and least objectionable to the mass of citizens, is military debt. We would lose our wealth if communism should ever occur in our country. We can make communism unpatriotic. If we make the citizens scared of the communists, and keep the citizens scared, we would have an excuse for a half-century of prosperity, and we could rake in profit. We could be careful to limit occasional skirmishes, refraining from intense war which would destroy our profits. "Cold War" might be a good name." Vietnam.

There is some thought that a few very rich people have exerted strong influence to get national debt almost endlessly continued at a planned rate by using dangerous bogey-man scare tactics. Mere Presidents could be pawns in such a game. The entire above paragraph is based on reasoning by coincidence, and therefore may be entirely or partly untrue. It could possibly be entirely true, and places the worst kind of ethical blame on use of the profit system.

You or I could easily make a very long list of conditions in which people or groups crunch against each other as a result of our economic system. A list of successes of the profit system could be made. Yet, it is not likely that many items on either list would lead to significant new principles even though many are subjects worthy of consideration. Most are like spokes of a wheel, having a common hub, the basics in Chapters 1 and 2. Most of the items of the list could be tied to factors such as unavoidable competition or inadequate increase in buying power within the system. Merely as examples, perhaps a dozen items of that kind will be breifly mentioned.

For instance, there is a definite dilemna in governmental regulation of business. Without regulation, some businesses ignore worker safety, consumer protection, etc. Too much regulation stifles the operation of the business maybe to the point of failure.

Union pressures, designed to give employees some balance of power when negotiating with a powerful business, often makes it difficult for the business to survive in the market place, especially international. Perhaps the scary part is that the mass of people accept this conflict situation as fate.

There is a large imbalance between the loyalty of employees to businesses and businesses to employees. Businesses treat employees as expendibles while employees use loyal service to earn a security niche. The larger the business, the greater seems the lack of loyalty to employees.

During times of deficient money increase, bringing hard times for business, massive reductions of work force are standard methods of decreasing expenses. The corresponding loss of market caused by unemployment of former employees seems to be ignored by businesses. Also, employees who have been jettisoned tend to ignore the market lack which forces businesses to make labor reductions. Suddenly placed in a precarious survival position, employees often feel personally betrayed by former employers. Both business and workers beg government to do something to correct difficulties. Full attention is paid to economic symptoms, none to system law causes.

Here is strong evidence that the general population has no awareness that we have and use a profit system that demands a system money increase. If people fail to supply adequate money increase, (debt increase) the profit system bebetrays all of the people.

As 1990 came, people became familiar with the phrase, "hostile takeover." A person, or a group, would acquire more than 50 percent ownership of a business. Through stock, which represents split ownership of a business, the take-over person or group would buy control of a company even against the wishes of the original owners. Very often, the purchased company, such as a big airline, had its assests sold by the take-over party. Sales of the assests would more than pay for the cost of take over, reaping gain for the person or group who initiated the take over. Sale of the assets gutted the unfortunate company, destroying it as a business concern. Employees, regardless of length of loyal service, found themselves dumped into unemployment.

Possibly the most evident factor showing in many takeovers is destruction. Building and enhancement of the business is not the object of a person or persons interested in quickly taking a big profit. Often, the take over person is not even working with his own money, but is merely manipulating the buying and selling of debt. Using bonds, (IOUs), as security, loans are acquired. Money from the loans is used to buy control of a company, the company assets are sold, and the loan repaid.

Because the goal is destruction, and crushing people underfoot during the process is common, the morality of the person doing the takeover is exposed. The action is openly exploitation. Naked jungle law is evident for all to see. Yet we ignore this use of jungle law tactics. Because jungle law lies just beneath the surface in normal use of the profit system, there is a bed of acceptance for the open jungle law shown during hostile takeovers. In this almost universal acceptance of cruelty we can see the result of long time use of profit system morality. People have been made nearly blind to immorality.

Multi-national corporations are those that do business in more than one country, like in the United States and also in Mexico. There are some clear indications that these corporations have no allegiance to some, or maybe to none, of the countries in which they do business.

The general objective is to hire labor at very low rates in one nation, then sell the products in another nation where labor rates are high and sale prices for the products can be high. Hidden is the results of money flowing from one area in the system and into another. Obvious is the failure to provide employment in the nation where the products are sold. There is exploitation of labor where the products are made. Labor people where the products are made can not afford the products. Unemployment in the high priced labor area depletes the market in that area. Markets stay low in both areas. This short sighted effort in futility defeats the manufacturer who uses it, and causes suffering in all areas.

In the last three or four decades, the labor force in the United States has been encountering increasing impermanence in chosen careers. The impermanence has increased to a level that is making the words "chosen career" almost meaningless. This impermanence results in anxiety, and maybe a bit of hysteria, in the work force as long range family planning, house buying, etc., become disrupted. The work force beginning to be included in this impermanence are management people. The owners of small business also suffer from the effects of impermanence, with life time planning and effort subject to being washed away.

The obvious impermanence surrounding

both labor and business people causes a backlash that acts adversely on the economic system. People are very reluctant to encumber themselves with long range debt when the immediate future is in doubt. This reluctance partly defeats the increase of debt which is necessary to make the profit system work. There are many omens to indicate the ever increasing difficulty in extending credit fast enough to meet the demands of our mature profit system.

The status of people, down through the ages, has often been set by the degree of wealth those people possessed. The way people behaved towards others, like applying the "golden rule", or being kind and altruistic, has also been used to set status. However, the amount of wealth possessed by someone has generally been the quickest way to status. Long ago, the number of slaves a person owned, even if those were treated with cruelty, determined status.

Our Constitution, with its message of all people treating all others fairly, has not succeeded in countering the use of the profit system. People strive hard for survival, then often ruthlessly strive for riches. Merely surviving is hardly acclaimed, but acheivement of wealth is praised. The profit system has taught us that people are generally to be graded on wealth and power, not consideration of others.

Equal application of law for all persons does not exist, even in the democracy enjoyed in the United States. People having great wealth not only are treated with great respect on a daily basis, but can hire attorneys to aid in getting advantage in law courts. People who are quite poor are not treated with great respect, and can demand far less rights than rich people in courts of law. The goals of democracy are subverted by disparity in wealth.

It appears to me that the majority of people, accustomed all their life to profit system practices, give their first loyalty to that economic system, and loyalty to democracy comes in a poor second. The confusion that seems to exist in equating democracy and the profit system perhaps comes from the freedom to change line of work, go into business, change to a different kind of business, etc. The thought is: private enterprise is free enterprise; democracy is freedom, so private enterprise is democracy. There is not only confusion of terms, but a bit of illusion in the foregoing thoughts.

A hard actuality is that for people suffering poverty, or for people just three or four pay checks away from poverty, freedom is near non existence. When it comes to the pursuit of life, liberty, and happiness, probably the most worthwhile set of papers in the world is the United States Constitution. Based on the Constitution, any one in the country is free to go to the moon and establish a home, or even a colony. Yet the granting of freedom to do something and the odds against making practcal use of that freedom generally depends upon control of sufficient wealth.

Even the right to free speech, guaranteed by the Constitution, can be subject to ownership of mass communication equipment. If the "media" is owned by the wealthy, then it will likely tend towards the opinions of the wealthy.

To head off future disaster, there needs to be a general awareness of how the profit system really works. There needs to be knowledge about what communism was and is really like, including the way dictatorships severely suppress people. Knowledge about economics must surmount, and where necessary, discard 200 year old teachings which have been with us so long that we have become rigidly convinced those teachings can not be wrong. Our survival rests on the growth of awareness of what is and what is not truth in the way we make our living. The means of communication, the "media", is necessary for awareness to occur before we reach the chaos stage of profit system self destruction. We are quite dependent on wealthy people who control the "media", sadly dependent upon the very people who may possibly feel inclined to squelch the necessary growth of economic awareness.

Mathematicians use terms such as "linear" and "non-linear" to describe the behavior of some change. The profit system's need for buying power increase is non-linear. It is therefor essential that the great mass of our population understands non-linear growth. Mathematicians amongst the population will readily understand non-linear change, but the large percentage of the population who do not consider themselves mathematicians must not be excluded from understanding. The problem of economic survival is ultimately in the hands of many non mathematicians.

Here is an analogy that might help understanding of progressive actions that are non-linear. Assume that a biologist places a single celled germ into a pure culture in which the single cell can live and reproduce. With a very powerful microscope, reproduction is observed. Assume that the cell splits once in 24 hours, forming two cells. In the next 24 hours, each of these two cells split, together forming four cells. This process doubles the number of cells each full day, becoming 8 cells, then 16, then 32, then 64, 128, 256, 512, 1024, 2048, 4096, 8192, 16384, and so on. At the end of the fourteenth day, there are 16384 cells.

This type of non-linear growth is called exponential growth. Because each germ cell in the culture is so tiny, the growth at the end of the fourteenth day might be very difficult to find, and seem quite unimpresive. Growth seems extremely slow. Yet, if we also look at this process as it nears its completion so we know its entire growth pattern, we may get a different understanding. Perhaps on the 124th day, we see that one sixteenth of the culture is covered with cell growth. On the 125th day, the growth covers one eighth of the culture. On the 126th day, growth covers one fourth. On the 127th day, cell growth will cover one half of the culture. This idea is important. In the very next 24 hours the growth will again double, and in so doing, will completely cover the culture.

Let us review. In the last four days of growth, the barely discernable 1/16th coverage suddenly becomes full growth. That last day of spectacular growth takes the culture from 1/2 coverage to complete growth.

Perhaps the preceding two paragraphs will give you an understanding of the last four pages of Chapter 2, if you missed understanding before now. Even if you understood it before, the explanation is placed here now for emphasis. The sudden swiftness of the profit system's yearly demand for money increase could easily catch us all unaware when the profit system is old enough. Like an avalanche, the demand will be overwhelming. No one is immune when the avalance comes. Our economic system has no conscience.

One summer day in 1931, two fifteen year old boys walked across a field of carrots. The field was perhaps 40 to 60 acres on irrigated land on the east side of California's San Joaquin Valley, a great farm area. The two boys reached the farm house just before the farmer came out to talk to 35 or 40 men.

"Men," the farmer said, "I can not hire you to harvest my carrot crop. I can not sell the carrots for the amount of money I would have to pay you to harvest them. I've been a farmer all my life, and it makes me physically sick to think of those carrots rotting in the field. You may take some home to your families. You may pull them and try to sell them, if you can find a buyer, but I can not lose more money paying you to harvest those carrots."

Your author knows about this because I was one of the two boys. As the two of us departed from the farm, I was very disturbed. The "Great Depression of 1929" had existed for two years. All up and down the highly productive valley huge quantities of food existed, but could not be sold. All up and down the valley men eager to work were unemployed. Families of unemployed men were hungry. The same condition existed across the entire United States. The question that stabbed me was, "With hungry people everywhere, all people in need, why can't the farmer sell all of his carrots?"

In Minnesota, dairy farmers poured fresh milk into the gutter. In citrus land California, oranges piled in warehouse size piles had kerosene sprayed on them to keep free oranges from destroying the low price of other oranges still offered for sale. Throughout the land, warehouses were full of unsaleable inventories. A universal symbol of the problem was the "CLOSED" signs on front gates of idle factories. Factories were closed while owners waited hopefully for the unemployed consumers to buy the overflow of goods. Clothing, hardware, new automobiles, farm machinery, and so forth without end, existed but could not be sold to people who were in need of all these items. With people in need, why could none of this be sold? The answer is in the early middle of Chapter 2.

In a profit system, when debt increase is insufficient to pay profit, there is an unsaleable surplus of goods equal in price to the total unacheivable profit. The unsaleable goods do not necessarily represent overproduction, but rather are goods that the profit system can not distribute when buying power increase is insufficient to pay profit. When the goods can not be distributed, then production stops, with labor and factories forced into idleness.

What can be said about the ethics of an economic system that creates unemployment, no markets for business and industrial people, severe hunger, lack of proper clothing, and inadequate housing amidst great abundance? If you can not question the ethics of the system, what can be said about the logic of using such a system? If you were too young to see and remember the suffering during the depression that started in 1929, Read John Steinbeck's "Grapes of Wrath". Nearly unbelievable to me was the almost stolid forebearance the suffering people showed for the severe and senseless hardship they endured.

SUMMARY

The way in which people make a living profoundly effects the behavior of people towards each other. Unavoidable, and also intentional, exploitation of any and all other people is the bedrock ethics of the profit system. Profit system ethics fosters economic dictatorship, which is restrained only slightly by political democracy. People have to survive inside the jungle law of the profit system, daily suffering alteration of their behavior. "Why don't you silly swimmers get yourselves a life boat?" Altruism working counter to jungle law is the proof of humanity's hidden greatness. This altruism alone is insufficient, and becoming increasingly futile. Exploitation taught by the constant pressures of profit system life is an ethic that is threatening to eliminate altruism. Even though each side needs the other, workers and business owners are forced to fight each other for a living share of business income. Workers are becoming expendible. Fully robotized factories would have no market. The quest for markets becomes international, leading to friction and maybe war between nations. A majority vote will not make the profit system work. It is futile to give loyal support to an economic system that will self destruct and strand all of its supporters. Overgrazing is the too long use of a once successful way of making a living. It is the comparative example of too long use of the profit system, to the point of disaster.

If an economic system allows each person full choice as to whether he abuses other people, then abuse is that person's unethical behavior. If the economic system allows no choice, but forces each person to abuse other people, then the economics system is unethical. The profit system is unethical. The great disaster is that people become abusive, taught by the profit system.

Chapter 4.
Soviet Communism, Ethics and Workability

In Chapter 1, we used pennies for cash buying power, IOUs for debt type of buying power, and described the basic arithmetic laws of profit system operation. In Chapter 2, it was concluded that the profit system process would reach an evntual impasse when no possible increase in buying power could any longer sustain the process. At that time, the profit system will self destruct, regardless of how numerous the people are who endeavor to sustain the system.

Knowing that our presently used economic system is going to fail regardless of how hard we try to save it, we must find a workable alternative method of production and distribution. The alternative to privately owned production and distribution for profit is publicly owned non profit production and distribution. Since we are being forced in the future to abandon the failing profit system, we must switch to a non profit system in order to survive.

Others before us have broken trail in setting up publicly owned production and distribution. The history of their efforts is quite dismal. Because we are forced to change, we would be well advised to study the efforts and failures that have gone ahead of us. Can we, for instance, look at Soviet Communism, learn from Soviet mistakes and contrive a workable and humane public enterprise?

At this point in this chapter, I feel like a person with a hang glider, ready to launch from a high precipice. It is a very scary situation. Below is a steep jumble of slopes, trees, and rocks. There are likely millions of pages written about Soviet Communism. I would like to have us move above the pages about communism, in the manner of a hang glider moving above the slope, trees, and rocks. We want to steer a route where we can look at the scenery, but not get tangled by obstructions.

The route I take is arbitrary, and maybe not the best. We will be looking for just enough significant views to see the overall picture of communism. You may want to do a lot of side reading.

To start, let me speak of four ideas, each one distinct from the other three. The four ideas are: first, democracy; second, dictatorship; third, private enterprise; and fourth, public enterprise. Some people seem to automatically hook these ideas together in two couplets as though they could be joined in no other combination. That is not so.

For us to effectively interpret our inspection of Soviet Communism, we should be able to consider the four ideas as separate, with various combinations possible. We can have private enterprise and democracy. We can have private enterprise and dictatorship. We can have public enterprise and dictatorship. We can have public enterprise and democracy. That last combination is what Soviet Communism tried to achieve, but failed to achieve.

Many persons writing about Soviet Communism start with the November, 1917

Russian Revolution. That revolution evolved into Soviet Communism, a dictatorial public enterprise. Using 1917 as a starting point seems like walking into the middle of a motion picture. Because the characters are not known, it is hard to follow the story.

Some important characters were the serfs. In the Russian Empire, serfs lived within the combination of dictatorship and private enterprise. Serfdom existed for generations, continuing into the century before communism. Serfs were essentially slaves, agricultural workers who were politically restricted from owning the land they worked.

The land owners were allowed to take a major portion of the crops raised by the serfs. Whatever part of the crops remained could be kept by the serfs. This may seem like the serfs were land renters. Agricultural land rental is familiar to us in the United States. The conditions for the Russian serfs were quite different from land rental in the United States. The serfs could not leave the land where they worked and take a job elsewhere. Serfs were permanent fixtures, like being part of the land to which they were assigned. The land owner, somewhat strangely, was not the direct owner of each serf in the way slaves are owned. The land owner could not sell the serfs away from the land. Yet, the land owner could sell all of the serfs along with the sale of the land worked by those serfs. The conditions for serfs was very nearly the same as slavery.

Additional important characters were the czars. The last few generations of czars were also known as emperors, for they ruled the large Russian Empire. One of the czar emperors was Alexander II, who became Emperor in 1855. In 1861, Emperor Alexander II, under pressure, emancipated all serfs in the Empire. Serfs were enabled to own land, and were even assisted in land purchase through state loans to be repaid by installment plan. We can note that freeing of Russian serfs took place about three years before slavery was abolished in the United States after our Civil War closed.

Another group of important characters were the peasants. Peasants were agricultural workers who were allowed to own and live on the land they worked. It would be a mistake to assume that peasants were wealthy land owners. For several reasons, land held by peasants was quite small. Horse drawn agricultural equipment was difficult to afford. Even when it could be bought, the equipment was crude. Agricultural work had to be done almost entirely by hand labor, severely limiting the amount of land that could be farmed even though women nearly doubled the work force. The limitations of hand labor is implicit in the familiar picture of women using a curved sickle to cut hand-held grain stalks.

When the serfs were freed, it was a big political step for them, but it was a very small financial step. They were free to join the peasants, living in poverty. A peasant family could produce little more than enough to sustain one family, but part of farm crops had to be shared with people who did not farm. This division of scarcity created a low standard of living. The entire Russian Empire lived within the limits set by hand labor farming.

Some more characters were the factory workers in the time between the free-ing of serfs and the 1917 Revolution. Factories in the Russian Empire were scarce and very unproductive compared to those in the United States, Great Brit-ian, Germany, and other industrially for-ward nations. The Russian Empire was somewhat isolated from the rest of the world, and isolation was fosterd by Rus-sian royalty. Backwardness was partly the result of isolation. However, there were increasing numbers of Russian fac-tory workers. Work conditions were atro-cious, and pay was poor. Poverty was the level for factory workers, a level maybe even less than that of the peasants. Per-haps factory workers, displaced from the land, had a less secure livelihood than peasants. That might partly account for their unrest, for they clamored for re-form. It was the factory workers, far more than the peasants, who talked revo-lution as the 1900's began.

Military people also were important characters. During the reign of the last three Russian Emperors, the army and navy fought wars. Wars were to conquer and subjugate other countries, expanding the empire. Wars were fought to keep subju-gated countries from winning freedom. The French, under Napolean, fought vainly to conquer Russia. Defensive war against

Japan was disaster for the Russians. Always, there were wars and more wars. Finally, there was defensive war against Germany when World War I started.

Russian rulers seem to have thought military manpower was very expendible. Perhaps the rulers tried hard to equip the miltary adequately, but the country's industrial output was too low. Fifteen million soldiers were placed on the battle line against Germany, but the soldiers lacked food, clothing, ammunition, and weapons. Never in any wars before did so many soldiers die.

Amongst all of the pre-revolutionary characters were the nobility, people with kinship to the czars. Blending with the nobility was the aristocracy, people of wealth. Most of the nobility owned extensive amounts of land and other forms of wealth. We can only guess whether the nobility was richer than the merchants, owners of industrial property, and bankers. We do know that Czar Nicholas II supported the rich people when industrial workers began talking economic revolution.

By 1900, the possibility of revolution was getting strong. Pushing people towards revolution was the extreme disparity between the rich and the vast number of poor. However, the wealth of the very rich people might have been tolerated except for two factors. First, the depth of poverty for most poor people was too close to non-survival. When considering the choice between nearly sure death by starvation, and possible death during rebellion, the risks of rebellion could easily seem the better choice. The second force that led towards revolution was the severity of repression of poor people by both the police and military controlled by the czar.

Starvation which threatened survival of the peasants and factory workers was aggravated by population increase. Low yield hand-labor agriculture and poor industrialization prior to 1900 produced goods that were increasingly insufficient as the population grew. It seems likely that population growth to a particular size set the time for revolution.

As inadequate national production fell further behind the needs of the growing population, rising demand for more equal distribution merely brought greater suppression of poor people. This rapidly rising ruthlessness of police and military triggered armed opposition. Just before World War I, revolution slowly began.

The growing revolutionary activity stopped in 1914 when World War I started. Faced by a foreign enemy, even the revolutionists joined the war effort. However, the war effort did not eliminate the basic causes from which revolution had started. As war continued, the economic inadequacy of the Russian Empire was made more evident. An empire that could not support its people during peace could not support both its civilians and the demands of war. Improperly supplied military people were being slaughtered by the foreign enemy, and the suffering of civilians greatly increased.

By February, 1917, riots in industrial cities renewed revolutionary activity, even though foreign war still raged. Years before, in 1905, military forces used bullets to stop marching unarmed men, women, and children asking for daily bread. Now, in the 1917 riots, military people disobeyed orders, refusing to fire on civilians, some armed. Czar Nicholas II was forced to abdicate, and the Russian Empire ceased to exist.

In March, a very loose temporary government was formed, pointed toward constitutional democracy. After eight months of aimless effort, lack of coordination, procrastination of vital decisions, and contention between factions, the provisional government was failing. This left unsolved the major problems leading toward revolution, and so a second, and major revolution, began in November.

As revolution renewed, many pressures tended to bring about growth of the Soviet style communism we have come to know. One factor is that the revolutionists were trying to do a twofold job. They were trying to go from a very lopsided distribution of wealth to a supposed equal distribution. They were also trying to jump Russia out of czarist imperialism and into democracy.

Legally, serfdom no longer existed after 1861. Practically, serfdom mentality was still present. Serfdom had existed for so many generations that people could not easily imagine life without aristocracy and a passively subservient poor class. The leap from serfdom and monarchy to publicly owned production and distribution under democracy was probably the largest social change ever tried.

Let us use the birth of democracy in America as a comparison to illustrate the two fold job facing the Russian revolutionists. Before the armed revolution, the colonists in America had long been developing the ideas that are the frame of democracy. Those colonists lived a self-reliant and independent life that nearly assured that democracy would eventually result. This was a far cry from the long standing serfdom and royalism in Russia, making democracy almost unthought of. Also, the American colonists, as they overthrew British rule, had no need to change from the then quite workable private enterprise system with which they were very familiar. In Russia, no one person, and certainly not the mass of people, knew what public ownership of production and distribution should be like. Few people within the Russian Empire understood the workings of democracy. Even fewer had faith that democratic methods had the strength needed for revolutionary change. Instead, many believed that a dictatorial military machine must be formed to accomplish the revolutionary economic goals.

The gun fire that ousted the Czar was followed by gun fire to oust the provisional government. Plans for a new government and new economic system were barely begun. About 150 million people were involved. As we trace the pressures and reaction of the people who built Soviet Communism, we should state a great lesson that is made evident. The lesson is that lots of planning is necessary to avoid chaos following a period of violent social disruption. We can also say, from observation, that starving people living under a tyrannical government, such as Czarist Russia, can hardly be expected to have opportunity to do essential planning before violence starts. This no-win situation resulted from the key factor, tyranny. Observe growth of the Union of Soviet Socialist Republics and you see a stacked deck of cards. The stacked deck brought poorly designed public enterprise with continuation of tyranny.

Not eveyone believed that dictatorship was necessary to accomplish the revolutionary economic goals. A few hoped that a constitutional democracy could be started. Some wanted democracy with a profit system, while others wanted democracy with public ownership of all production and distribution. A strong pressure tending to defeat democracy was the need for haste. A move had to be made quickly to some effective government and economic system or else great numbers of people would starve to death during the transition.

Opposing the need for speed was resistance by the mass of people. The revolution had only partly been a people's movement. Actively, and to a greater degree passively, the people had overthrown an oppressive government. Yet, they knew not where they were going next. Not having clear plans beyond overthrow of tyranny, the vast majority of people drifted.

Times of social chaos and disasterous delay foster dictatorship. Pushed by desperation and lured by hopes of a unifying direction, people may fall into a trap. If any one with a plan for action comes along, that person may become a leader people will follow a bit blindly, unaware of a possible great danger.

The huge population of the former Russian Empire was in a desperate situation. The provisional government, made up by what we might term as comittees, had been inept. Under the leadership of Vladimir Ilich Lenin, the Bolsheviks had been the ones to overthrow the provisional government. The huge and desperate population followed Lenin, some actively, but most very passively and reluctantly.

In a former paragraph, plus this last one, there is the implication that Lenin was deliberately trapping the population into danger. That he was doing it deliberately is not the truth. Lenin was a very idealistic man. From the age of about seventeen, he set himself against tyranny. As a university student, he became active against what he considered as exploitation of peasants and workers by the rich aristocracy. After Lenin received a law degree at Saint Petersburg University, he became an active Marxist. It became Lenin's goal to create a society free of both governmental and economic tyranny. During political exile in Siberia, he began writing books. Later, during self imposed exile outside of Russian restraint, he wrote more books and was active in political and economic theory groups. When Lenin became head of the new government in Russia after the 1917 revolution, he still aimed at creation of a classless society. He believed that his policies would eventually greatly benefit mankind. He was not after unlimited personal power and wealth. However, Lenin was a revolutionist.

Very often, revolutionists believe that the ends justify the means. Lenin believed that. His policies included armed overthrow of any opposition as he and his group established a worker's temporary dictatorship to usher in public ownership of production and distribution. It was Lenin's avowed belief that after it had served its purpose, the worker's dictatorship would wither away, leaving only a very minimum of political coercion. The belief was that socialized, or publicly owned, production and distibution would make most laws and coercion unnecessary. Even though he was its chief director, Lenin seems to have thought of himself as only one of a mass of workers using a dictatorship that would exist only briefly.

Perhaps we should grant that some leaders of the revolution thought of themselves as benevolent dictators, if such is possible. They may have believed they were only holding dictatorial powers in trust, ready to relinquish power to the masses of people when those people had sufficiently learned about democracy and about managing publicly owned production and distribution. We do not have to grant that benevolent large scale dictatorships can easily exist.

Historically, dictatorships follow a path far from benevolence. I feel that we can not understand the ethics and failures of Soviet Communism unless we understand the normal patterns of dictatorship.

Dictatorship is, or becomes, self serving. There are few people such as Lenin, people who can refrain from using dictatorial power for personal power and increase of personal wealth. Even if some top leader is able to remain immune to greed and thirst for power, a dictatorship involves many other people who do scramble for power and wealth. Dictatorships tend to intensify in severity and in scope. Increase in severity occurs when opposition is encountered. Dissidents outside of the dictatorship are eliminated, and purged within the dictatorship. To counter possibility of overthrow, the numbers within the dictatorship are limited to a minimum, while the base of control outside is always expanded as much as possible. Rigid rules are set to keep control intact.

Initiative and creativity can appear to be dissent, so it is squelched. Mass brain power, or the mutual assistance to thinking that can occur in cooperative teamwork, has to be stifled lest it lead to group opposition to the dictatorship. Every thought that anyone has must be regimented into a narrow channel, fully loyal to maintenance of the dictatorship. The effort of all of this causes a dictatorship to become ever more complicated, inflexible, and cumbersome. Use of secret police to protect the dictators is a standard method. Power necessarily granted to secret police is feared by the dictators, with takeover always possible by secret police. Insecurity within the dictatorial group defeats planning and accomplishment. Then there is lying, propoganda repeated endlessly until the hearer believes it and tellers nearly do. A peculiar blindness develops. Reality is destroyed until there is no true basis for decision making. The effort needed to maintain a dictatorship leaves little time for benevolence or solving of problems for the benefit of the masses of people outside the dictatorial group. Dictatorships almost never voluntarily relinquish their control. However, dictatorships always self-destruct over a long enough period of time.

Even though dictatorships are extremely anti-mankind, Lenin used the worker's dictatorship as the method of government when he became leader after the November revolution. I feel that when Lenin set up dictatorship, entrapped by the fallacy of any means to a highly desirable end, he was not far sighted enough to see he was irrevocably defeating his own ultimate goal. For dictatorship to survive, it must follow patterns which pressure a dictator along a set path. The hands of even a most benevolent dictator are tied.

Perhaps 150 million people faced starvation as a result of the social disruption from the revolution, added to severe poverty before. This vast suffering population did not quickly embrace Lenin nor his worker's dictatorship with its program of untried public production and distribution. The welfare of this mass of people was the goal of the dictatorship, but to move toward the goal, that mass had to be forced to learn and accept the new ways of life. Opposition, and even dissidence, within the masses could not be tolerated and had to be purged. While purging and re-education proceeded, that mass of people had to be kept alive. That's a contradiction.

Some paragraphs back, it was written that a dictatorhip could not spend the effort to do much for the welfare of people. As a prime example that dictatorships must disregard people's welfare, the new dictatorship quickly became involved in civil war. Named Congress of the Russian Communist Party in 1918, Lenin's group was openly opposed by some people. A chief objection was Lenin's World War I peace treaty with Germany in March, 1918. A powerful group, the White Russians, tried to knock out Lenin's Red Russian government. For the new dictatorship to survive, it had to shift its main attention to the civil war. That brought near abandonment of the dire problems of the huge population.

During civil war, lasting a bit more than two years, the government made little improvement in agricultural production and industrialization. Before the civil war started, the Congress decreed, "The right to private land is annulled forever.......The landlord's property in the land is annulled immediately and without any indemnity whatever." A long acting and troublesome exemption was made. Poor peasants and the Cossack rank and file were specifically allowed to retain their holdings, but were limited to one and a quarter acres. The land of big estates and of churchs was made national property and placed under temporary control of local peasant committees. Hired labor on any land was prohibited. Congress stated, "The use of the land must be equalized, that is, the land is to be divided among the toilers according to local conditions on the basis of standards either of labor or consumption." This last decree was vague, and subject to much local interpretation.

When civil war began, the great masses of the population were left to provide for themselves. While providing for themselves, they were burdened with civil war demands for food and equipment. Local committees of peasants assuming control of large hodings of land tended to deny anyone use of those large holdings. This excluded great amounts of land from production although that production was sorely needed.

In a country so vast, there were numerous different ethnic groups, with more than 150 languages. Each group did things its own way, relying on centuries of habit. Local peasant comittees felt authorized to set up local dictatorships. Throughout the nation, the rules of one group seldom conformed to the rules of any other group. This made a fractured social order, slow to mend and build anew. Greater suffering and death came from this disunity. Yet, those that survived perhaps did so by doing the things they had for generations. They farmed their tiny plots of land, still not national property.

During the civil war, which lasted from early 1918 until March, 1921, agriculture was far from being nationally owned production and distribution. Agriculture was carried out mostly on very small sized private land by people who were working for personal survival, first, and private profit if there was any excess to sell.

Since agricultural people made up most of the population, the country was not communist nor socialist. It remained basically a private enterprise profit system. As civil war ended, Lenin found that he had the Russian Bear by the tail. He couldn't let go, and he couldn't make the massive population suddenly shift to full public ownership, production, and distribution. Even though nationalization of factories had been started by industrial workers, those workers were only a minority of the population. The severity of famine across the entire nation was such that Lenin could not risk the attempt to force immediate communism. Lenin decreed a temporary continuation of profit system private enterprise, including changing some industry back to capitalism. These changes were called the New Economic Policy.

Outside reading is again recommended, with the suggestion that you note that many profit system methods, such as wages, piece work pay, finance at interest rates, etc., were continued throughout the life of Soviet Communism.

Lenin's group named themselves the Communist Party. For the first time, they were in a position of control solid enough to begin to expand their aims. We should note that the name for the group was not the Socialist Party. As the Communist Party, Lenin and his group acknowledged that they were only a transitional group. The Communist Party hoped to someday create socialism, supposedly superior to communism.

It seems like the right time to talk about the stated and implied goals of Lenin and his followers. By considering what they hoped to acheive, we can judge the degree of failure, and guess about reasons for that failure. One significant reason so far was that historical conditions had made it impossible to plan enough in advance to avoid chaos.

The Communist Party hoped to start a long string of changes that would evolve into socialism. In general terms used then, socialism would be a classless society. Major production and distribution would be publicly owned. Nearly all property, excluding personal, would be publicly owned.

Beyond material conditions, other conditions of life were considered the aim of socialism. A list would include such things as the right to work, no poverty, health care, mobility, equality of income, pensions, and an equitable share of wealth, to list only a few. Exploitation of one person by another would no longer exist. Physical force coercion, and other forms of coercion, would not exist. It was expected that the dissolution of private property rights would obviate the need for most laws. "The administration of things and the direction of the processes of production" would replace the present "government over persons." Two very important general goals are freedom from jungle law, and freedom from fear. I do not believe these two were ever listed by Lenin. However, I feel they were implied from other general and specific goals. Freedom from fear is a success or failure indicator that is most easy to monitor.

All of these specific and general goals are appropriate for us to judge for success in attainment, or failure to achieve.

As a preview to judging success or failure of Soviet Communism, I feel we can state some huge doubts that there was ever any posibility of success. This is definitely a hindsight, second-guessing type of statement, for we were not present with Lenin in 1921 to make a forward looking prediction of failure. We do not know that any of socialism's goals were possible to achieve by any means. Yet, we have opportunity here to point out that when socialism teamed with dictatorship, it rather certainly became incapable of bringing about the goals aimed at by socialism. For socialism to achieve its goals would have required two or three generations of leaders with a base of democracy and a delicacy of understanding people, a sensitivity to both the physical and emotional needs of people. It would have required great ability in management of things.

The brutish nature of dictatorship made it hostile to any possible success of socialism. Lenin was the head of a government made up of mostly elected people. We could wrongly think that the government was a democracy. The electors were the workers and the peasants, a designation that was peculiarly Russian. The workers and the peasants chose representatives, called soviets, or councils, or committees, then chose Lenin as top head of the government. Those councils also chose Lenin's main aides. This surely has the appearance of democracy, but it is only half-truth. The other half of the truth is that the source of decisions was Lenin.

The direction of flow of orders is what determines the existence of dictatorship or of democracy. If the workers and peasants had told the elected council, the soviets, what to do, and the soviets had told Lenin what to do, then there would have been democracy. Instead, Lenin told the council what to do and the council told the workers and peasants what to do. In reality, the soviets were the organization by which dictator's orders were disseminated to the workers and peasants.

Even if we grant that the top aides, the most powerful members of the council, could influence decisions made by Lenin, Soviet Communism began and continued as a dictatorship.

To make sure that the soviets were ruled by the top leaders, the Communist Party was formed. With membership limited to the dictatorial group, the Communist Party took control of the soviets. New membership into the Party was restricted to people approved by party leaders. This insured that the dictators retained control. We can assume that during the consolidation of the dictatorship, the economic welfare of the nation's population was of secondary importance. Even Lenin was likely diverted from badly needed economic organization of the country. Thus, the dictatorship began to disclose its true nature by showing that the people did not come first. Lenin never did reverse, probably could not reverse, neglect of the people by the dictatorship.

In 1924, a new Constitution was written, and the name of Union of Soviet Socialist Republics was taken.

Amongst the most powerful assistants to Lenin were two men, Leon Trotsky and Joseph Stalin. There was intense rivalry between Trotsky and Stalin. In the midst of this rivalry, Lenin died in January, 1924. His death disclosed another phase of dictatorship: power struggle to succeed to top position within the dictatorship. Again, during this power struggle, the economic welfare of the vast population was not the most important considerration. The people were neglected during the four years it took Stalin to remove Trotsky and some other opposition leaders. During the last of 1927 and the first of 1928, Stalin began a pattern of intense repression. He had tens of thousands of former opponents exiled to Siberia and Northern European Russia.

We look at a man who supposedly had the most humanitarian aims. Stalin seemingly fought, worked and contrived to create socialsm and its expected great benefits for his nation, if not all mankind. At least, Stalin professed to be trying to create socialsm and its goals. We can not doubt Stalin's actions of political oppression were inconsistent with his stated socialist goals. We can only guess whether Stalin was telling a huge lie to gain support for personal power, or was deluded by the idea that the ends justified any means.

When Lenin died, he left alive the dictatorship he had started. I feel that the almost inevitable pattern through which a dictatorship progresses assured the eventual destruction of all of Lenin's idealistic goals. I feel that the sowing of the seeds of dictatorship by Lenin made a mockery of his life and betrayed his people. No carefully contrived fictional Greek tragedy could equal the true futility of Lenin's efforts.

It is not proper for us to imply that there was any certainty that socialism would reach its goals even if a dictatorship had not been dragging it down. The theory of socialism as Lenin's group envisioned it might have been seriously flawed.

Factors other than the weight of dictatorship placed a heavy load on the transition to socialist goals. Involving more than 150 million people, the Soviet Communist effort was the most massive social movement of all history. Huge numbers of people do not easily change their way of life. The time and location setting for the huge social experiment involved people burdened with centuries of accepting subservience as the only way of life. The strength of this subservience was shown when Stalin exiled tens of thousands of people to nothern Siberia. More than 150 million people condoned his oppressive actions.

Soon after Stalin exiled his opponents, he must have felt a bit secure. He took enough time out from the power struggle to set up an economic five year plan. In 1928, eleven years after the Bolshevik Revolution, the country still was mostly using a badly disorganized private enterprise. Transportation and some industry was publicly owned and operated, but little else was. The five year plan was to increase and organize public ownership within the nation's economy.

With the five year economic plan barely started, Stalin returned to the affairs of dictatorship, making his position ever firmer. In 1929, he was openly considered supreme ruler of the country. In 1930, Stalin strongly mixed dictatorship and economics by ruthlessly forcing most peasant families into state owned collective farming.

Ever since the 1917 Revolution, peasant families had privately owned their tiny farms. Thousands of people who had owned vast acerage had been forced to give all their land to the state. The peasants had been specifically excluded from having to surrender their land. Some land from the huge former estates was divided up to be given to peasant families. This was equalized private enterprise, not public ownership. Now, the first five year plan was calling for most preasants to surrender their land to become consolidated into the collective farms.

The peasants were probably torn between their age old habit of subservience and fear that they were losing the only thing they could rely on for survival: their small bits of land. Apparently, the peasants had no faith in the newly forming channels of food distribution from collective farms. Maybe there was a deep lack of trust in the practicality of the collective farms. Probably fearing that giving up their land meant death, millions of peasant families rebelled. The peasants did not realize that refusal to give up their land could also mean death. Rebellion took the form of destruction of immense quantities of live stock and grain. Stalin had thousands of rebellious peasants shot. Hundreds of thousaands more were exiled to the northern parts of Siberia and European Russia.

Before the confiscation of peasant lands, before the massive destruction of food, and before the removal of hundreds of thousands of agricultural workers, the nation teetered on starvation. After agricultural activity had been totally upset, there was famine. This resulted in several million deaths from both starvation and disease.

Although construction of large scale industry was one goal of the first five year plan, significant output of agricultural machinery had to wait for the seccond five year plan. During the first five year plan, as peasants were forced to give up their small farms, there was insufficient machinery to work large sized collective farms. Do you agree with me in saying that Stalin decreed actions in a sequence that could not be physically accomplished? Making peasant farms collective should have followed the second five year plan output of agricultural machinery. We can not prove this assumption, but peasants might have willingly contributed their bits of land to form large sized collective farms if they knew the large farms would be sufficiently mechanized. Dictators, deeply involved in dictatorship, make very poor managers. They are prone to make economic decisions rather than achieve solutions based on reality.

If Stalin did not know he had caused millions of deaths, he could be unaware only if he was too inconsiderate of human life to see what he had done. If Stalin did know he had caused the deaths, he showed very low regard for human life. Either way, this example showed that dictators make very poor custodians of people's lives. The longer a dictator is in power, and the stronger the dictator is, the less conscience he shows in his treatment of people.

One man who is a dictator can directly, obviously, and severely damage the economy of his country. A dictator can also indirectly severely damage the economy. This occurs through the damaging effect the dictator has on the attitudes and behavior of the population.

After all of the damage that Stalin

caused during the first five year plan, he turned his attention to making his dictatorship more complete. During the second five year plan, he began a long continued strengthening of his secret police. He also began a very unusual purge. Strangely, the purge was not to kill obvious opponents. Instead, it was to eliminate all long time leaders of the revolution and civil war, people who might seem to have been Stalin's friends.

It is likely that no one knows why Stalin purged people with whom he had been allied. One person's guess was that Stalin wanted to impress the population with how tight the dictatorship would be.

Here are a couple of guesses of my own. Maybe Stalin wanted to rid himself of any obligation to share policy making. Your enemies can not ask you for favors. Neither can your friends, if they are dead. The second guess is that Stalin wanted to eliminate any and all future criticism. You can not appear to be perfect with a bunch of critics sounding off. Stalin had at least one huge mistake to cover up. That was the improperly sequenced attempt to force collective farming before machinery was ready to make large farming possible. Perhaps as Stalin rid himself of possible finger pointers, he could also have dead scapegoats whom he could blame for past mistakes.

While most of Stalin's "friends" were being purged, the way citizens felt about Stalin's dictatorship underwent a very significant transformation that seems illogical, on the surface.

Before the purge, most citizens may have condoned and tolerated dictatorship although they greatly resented it. Most citizens may have even been aware that other people also disliked the dictatorship. Whatever Stalin's reason for the purge, as it continued, a deep fear affected the people. First it brought a halt to any overt or voiced disapproval of the dictatorship. Absence of open disapproval led each citizen to think that all other people approved of the dictatorship. Isolated from each other by silence, the people of the nation flipped from passive opposition to active, if pretended, support of Stalin's dictatorship.

As the outward behavior of the people changed, a peculiar additional change began. Pretended support for Stalin became actual support. The attitude of the population changed. The depth, range, and speed of the transformation is amazing. Within perhaps 2 or 3 years, as fear from the purges seperated individuals, people not only openly approved of Stalin, but worship began. That misplaced worship remained throughout the rest of Stalin's life. The worshippers seemed to ignore or never realize that Stalin was an unequalled mass murderer. Can this blindness to reality be explained by the tendency of people to sanctify viciousness in order to clear themselves from the guilt of condonement?

About this page of this book, some readers may wonder if this book is about economics or the social psychology of dictatorships. Next to war, dictatorships are second in the power of their adverse effect on economics.

One feature about how dictatorships develop has not yet been sufficiently emphasized. It is my feeling that dictatorships develop in three stages. In the first stage a dictator achieves physical control over a group, but is not yet secure. The dictator then bans dissent, which triggers the second stage by dividing the individuals of the group, making them betray each other. The individuals of the group perform the third stage by each believing that all other people in the group fully support the dictatorship.

We have been looking for mistakes made by Soviet Communism. We see that an indirect result of using dictatorship can be devastating. Dictatorship wrecks the people. By condonement of the dictator's actions, the people become guilty of complicity in any human atrocities the dictator orders.

After the third stage of dictatorship was complete, the people took over the constant police effort which assured continuation of the dictatorship. Each individual remained afraid to condone any dissent by any other individuals. This made every individual a helper of the secret police, stifling opposition. But each person also lived in a pervasive and constant fear of all other citizens and secret police. All living in fear shows social system failure. This failure of Soviet Communism became the daily condition of life. Behind the face of any person, there could have been a secret police agent. As a reminder, purges of untold numbers of people continued as long as Stalin lived.

Before the second five year economics plan was ended, the people of the Soviet Union were presenting a uniform face to foreign nations. The people appeared solidly patriotic, all believing in the ideology of Soviet Communism, and strongly in favor of Stalin's dictatorship.

Acceptance of Stalin by the population made them very gullible when he lied to them. Stalin greatly exaggerated any success, whatever the subject, but minimized or kept secret any poor performance or failures. The web of lies, secrecy, and fear destroyed appropriate reaction to reality, laying a foundation for incorrect and very harmful decisions in the nation's production and distribution.

According to numerous implications so far in this book, Soviet Communism could not succeed at anything but famine, with Stalin lying about everything. Contrary to the implications, Soviet Communism was somewhat productive during the first five year plan. Even greater production occured during the second five year plan. Perhaps the squelching effect of dictatorship had not yet set in by the middle of the second five year plan. At that time, Stalin's purge of his former allies became intense. Until then the dictatorship may have provided a unified and even coordinated economic effort, slightly proving that production could occur through use of public ownership.

During the second five year plan, considerable advances made in heavy industry improved economic conditions in general, although agriculture still lagged. As the economy moved out of chaos and into growing achievement, the population had a period of rising spirits and pride in their nation. Much of the nation's production was diverted to increase the size of defensive military capability. There was enough production for some consumer goods, although scarcity still existed for consumers. In spite of a lack of abundance in consumer goods, the total rise in production gives us some insight into the potential capability of publicly owned production and distribution, even hampered by dictators.

This is an important item for consideration by us since we are intensely interested in the possibility that public enterprise can save us when the profit system does collapse. Sad to say, we are treated to an all too brief view of promising productivity in the Soviet Union. The secrecy and lies inherent in dictatorship obscured and distorted our view during the rest of Stalin's life.

In spite of exaggerated claims, the second five year plan was actually great enough to make the Soviets optimistic. In 1938, the third five year plan was begun with the avowed goal of making Soviet Communism the world leader in economic productivity, both in quantity and excellence.

In comparison, the year of 1938 found the United States slowly recovering from several years of the most severe economic depression of its history. The Great Depression, starting in 1929, exhibited great abundance that could not be sold because buying power increase had fallen far behind the amount demanded by a very productive profit system. Stalin had at least a plausible part truth base for his claim that Soviet Communism was superior to capitalism. Increases in production under communism would not result in the profit system paradox of abundance amidst depression.

In 1939, Stalin and Germany's dictator, Adolf Hitler, made a pact of non aggression. One of the conditions of the pact was that the Soviets would furnish grain and other materials to the Germans. To me, there is some appearance of extortion, but that is not part of what we are looking for. The point of interest is that the Soviet Union had enough agricultural and other production to spare large amounts in 1939, one year into the third five year plan. We can suspect that the population of the Soviet Union suffered continued scarcity, that their welfare was sacrificed to Stalin's foreign policy.

Adolf Hitler, the fascist dictator of Germany, did not allow the Soviet's third five year plan to run its course. German Fascism was a very imperialistic dictatorial private enterprise. By its nature, it was antagonistic to communism. Nazi was the name Hitler applied to his social system, which meant National Socialism. The word socialism was a catch word lie, for public ownership was not a goal. Hitler also lied to Stalin when he promised that German troops would never invade any territory of the Soviet Union.

Strangely, Stalin believed the lie. Hitler broke his promise in June, 1941, when Nazi soldiers did invade the Soviet Union. Stalin and other Soviet leaders learned a lesson about the treachery and destructiveness of dictatorships.

Even during peace, it had been difficult to assess the economic capability of Soviet Communism. When World War II struck the Soviet Union, it became nearly impossible to evaluate the benefit or harm of using Soviet type public ownership of production and distribution. For the duration of World War II, total disruption of the Soviet third five year plan occured.

Some war history needs coverage because war caused Soviet material and people losses so great that it is hard to imagine. For about three years, as the invaders penetrated deeply into Russia and were finally ejected, both the invaders and defenders destroyed and "scorched the earth". The invaders were notably destructive of factories and other industrial capability. The loss of Soviet soldiers and civilians was in the millions. As the Soviets forced retreat of the Nazis, hundreds of thousands of Nazi captives were placed in forced labor camps, working for the Soviets.

The Soviets fought the retreating Nazi all the way back to Berlin. There are reports that Soviet generals were amazed to find the living standard higher in war torn foreign countries than it had been in the pre-war Soviet Union. This small comparison gives us a rough measurement of Soviet low living standards and depth of gullibility of the Soviet people before the war.

The European part of World War II ended on May 9, 1945. The Soviets then turned to aiding the United States against the Japanese in the last part of World War II. Soviets occupied most of Manchuria and Northern Korea. The war was ended by United States atomic bombs against Japan, and the Soviet Union was considered one of the great military powers of the world. The living standard of the Soviet population was still low.

The Soviet Union occupied a large area of industrial Europe, as far west as Berlin. The Soviets set up the "iron curtain" around the boundaries of the area occupied by them. Using reparations, the big name for spoils of war, the Soviets tried to aid in repairing their very badly damaged country. Within the occupied areas, the Soviets dismantled entire industrial plants, moving these east into war devasted areas of the Soviet Union. Millions of German prisoners of war continued to be placed in forced labor camps in the Soviet Union.

Within a couple of years, the Soviet Union was acknowledged to be the second most productive nation in the world. That makes it seem that Soviet Communism was a great success. The economics ranking can be questioned. With all the secrecy routinely used by the Soviet Union, how can anyone know that the second place ranking in economics was really so? A second question is about efficiency. Perhaps the second place rating was only because the country was so geographically large. A tiny farm may produce much more per acre than a giant one, yet the total output of the giant farm may far outstrip the tiny farm. What counts is the living standard, not total production. Even with Soviet secrecy, there were rumors that the living standard was low.

The post World War II period was one of great prosperity for the United States. That prosperity resulted from a tremendous infusion of buying power in the form of war time national debt. In a round about way, that greatly affected the economics situation of the ordinary citizen of the Soviet Union. Josef Stalin had been a war time ally of the United States, but he seems to have feared the prosperous United States once war was over. Stalin increased Soviet arms at the expense of Soviet consumers.

Some fear of the United States had a firm basis. Stalin knew that people in the United States were objecting to the Soviet post-war territorial expansion. Because of Soviet expansion, many people in the United States also had fear. From this mutual distrust, both the Soviets and the United States started an armament race known as the cold war. There is also some possibility that some people in the United States urged debt purchasing of armament to feed United States prosperity.

The cold war greatly influenced the living standards of both the United States and the Soviet Union. Regardless of the drain on the economy, and failure to produce consumer goods, the Soviets strived to produce intercontinental ballistic missiles carrying nuclear warheads. In the United States, the same armament effort was made. Both nations succeeded, though costs were high. One unbalance soon occured. In the United States, the arms race was financed with credit, or debt. That financing flowed into the economy of the nation as buying power, giving the United States continuing prosperity that resulted in a rising standard of living for consumers. In the Soviet Union, diversion of productivity into costly armament kept the Soviet citizens from sharing the productivity. A low living standard resulted.

In 1917, Vladimir Ilich Lenin and others had visions of converting the former Russian Empire into socialism. One of the goals of socialism was to create a coopeative public ownership of production and distribution with an output so high that poverty no longer existed for anyone. Thirty years later, in 1950, Soviet Communism still had not eliminated poverty. What caused continuation of subsistence level poverty in one of the world's largest nations?

We are trying to separate the effects of a political system from the results of a method of economics. Was it possible that people risked starvation by simply refusing to produce? Or could it be that dictatorship mangled the production process so badly that the vast population could barely feed themselves? To feed an insatiable military machine, perhaps the dictatorship planned the wrong kind of production. The Soviet people could not eat military hardware.

In spite of the blanket of secrecy over the Soviet Union, we know that the people did produce, and in large quantity. The dictatorship did mismanage production. Its mismanagement was twofold. One mismanagement was in choice of what to produce. The other mismanagment factor will be written about, later. The size and nature of the military machine was no secret, for it was flaunted. Nuclear warheads on intercontinental ballistic missiles were produced so bountifully that they assured destruction of more than one major possible enemy. Then this arms quantity was doubled, then remultipled several times, all to the point of absurdity. Of course, the armament absurdity meant continued mere subsistence poverty for the consumers of the nation. The dictatorship was almost entirely to blame for Soviet poverty, and also for burdening Soviet citizens with endless fear of other nations. This is so obvious that we could be reasonably sure without delving further.

It may be useful to add to the picture so that we can recognize and avoid certain patterns found in dictatorship. In the last few years before Stalin's death in 1953, the output of publicly owned production was limited by people who became managers solely because they were Communist Party members.

Hoping to achieve membership in the Communist Party, a person had to start as a child, grauduating through successive stages of Communist Party ideology. Seemingly, a prime requirement to moving from stage to stage was complete conformity with ideological teachings. Reaching adulthood, membership in the Communist Party was allowed. Children not choosing early to try for membership were later almost surely excluded from membership. Candidates for Communist Party membership were not required to attain technical knowledge in areas such as industry, construction, transportation, engineering, communication, medicine, agriculture, management, or science.

A Communist Party member without technical skill in industry could expect probable assignment to a management position in any part of the nation's economy, for instance as manager of a factory. With no background training or experience, such managers made decisions that likely were mediocre, and often destructive of productive capability. Such faulty management by inept Party members often occured in all important areas of economic effort. It is easy to see that mismanagement by the dictatorship seriously impaired production, greatly decreasing the living standard of the nation.

Destruction of morale occured when technically inept Party members became managers in any area where technical ability was needed. Capable workers, limited from becoming managers, had to suffer faulty decisions by managers who held positions of authority only because they were Party members. Workers must have cringed when they were forced to exert effort that they knew was wasted by poor management.

Thinking is not fostered by adherence to set doctrine. Thinking ability was likely impaired amongst Communist Party members whose chief qualification was life-long rigid conformity to Party doctrine. The nation suffered because of this low ceiling placed on the level of thinking.

Low morale was bad enough, with unhappy people and low production. But that was the least of the problem. If we remember that we are talking about dictatorship, we see that a factory manager was much more than just an inept boss. He represented the dictatorship. For safety's sake, each worker would tend to remain as anonymous as possible, refraining from activity that brought excess attention to himself. High personal achievement was very risky, as was being part of an inspirationally productive group. In a multitude of ways, the Soviet dictatorship crushed creativity, leaving robot-like minimum compliance and a very high rate of alcoholism. A lot of human spirit must have been forced into dormancy.

It seems to be a contradiction that a constituion existed for the Union of Soviet Socialist Republics during the entire time that Stalin was dictator. One was written in Lenin's time, rewritten in 1924, and was replaced by another written in 1936, seventeen years before Stalin died. Each had features to establish a legislative body elected by the population and responsive to the population. If the dictatorship had allowed the constitution to take effect, there would have been no dictatorship.

Why the 1936 constitution, written with permission of the dictatorship? First, Stalin engaged in farce, making believe to the population of the nation. Second, a significant amount of the constitution formed the agreement between the individual Soviet Republics, defining and enabling the Union.

In this chapter, the idea has been presented that Soviet Communism was almost entirely publicly owned production and distribution. The 1936 Constitution defined banking, with loans. It dealt with taxation. It continued the general rules by which industry, agriculture, and other public enterprise opeated in a manner much like profit system private enterprise groups.

That is a tangle of wording. Communism, socialism, private enterprise, public enterprise, even democracy or dictatorship, all are words with fuzzy meanings for different people. Maybe some comparisons should be made with familiar activities in the United States.

Across the United States, we have a system of public highways on publicly owned land, built with public money, and used by the public. With some degree of clarity, that highway system can be called public enterprise. We can look a bit deeper, and see that the public money is a pool created by taxation. Taxation requires that individuals and companies pay money to be placed into the public money pool. Taxation is the link between public enterprise highways and private enterprise companies and individuals.

Publicly owned parks, such as Yellowstone, Yosemite, etc., are on publicly owned land. Like the highway system, the parks are maintained by public money raised by taxation. Within the parks, there are often private enterprise operations known as concessions. For example, small fast food service buildings, built and equipped by private investors, sit on publicly owned land. For the privilege of an exclusive market in which to sell hot dogs, hamburgers, and soft drinks, the owners of the fast food service pay a fee to the appropriate governmental agency. This is private enterprise on public land.

This last example seems somewhat similar to the operational methods of the collective farms during Stalin's dictatorship. Farm workers banded together in a cooperative effort to raise crops on publicly owned land. For the privilege of using public land, a collective farm was required to sell a quota amount of the crop to the Soviet government at a price set by the government. The government stores then sold the farm crop quota to consumers.

Money that the government paid to the collective farm for the quota was used by the farm manager to pay the collective farm workers. Any crop yield greater than the required quota could be sold by the collective farm group to any available buyer. Whether the manager of the farm split this extra money with the workers is not known. We do recognize that this entire collective farm operation is strikingly similar to a profit system operation in the United States.

During Stalin's days, the farm worker's pay did not continue during the farming off-season. Neither was each worker's pay necessarily the same amount received by other members of the collective. It was not necessarily the same pay received by members of different collective farms. I could find no references to show that, in order to exist all year, farm workers had to find off-season jobs other than farming. I may be unfair in thinking that many workers had to "shift for themselves", and that Soviet Communism may have left families in precarious conditions at times.

The collectives rented tractors and other farm equipmenet from tractor "stations". Probably almost no peasants, familiar with hand labor only, were ready to care for tractors. The tractor stations seemingly bought the tractors from tractor factories, maybe with loans, at interest, from the government bank. The rental rates for the tractors had to be high enough to purchase tractors, keep them in repair, replace them with newer ones, pay loans, and net enough money to also pay the tractor station personnel.

Does all of this sound a lot like a profit system private enterprise operation? There seem to be many areas in which Soviet Communism resembled a profit system more than communism. Established in 1921, the State Bank headed all banks, all owned and operated by the government. The State Bank issued currency and extended short-term credit to industrial and agricultural enterpises. Lesser banks extended long-term credit in agricultural, industrial, commercial and municipal finance. We note, for example, that the government did not pay for such things as factories and factory equipment. The government granted loans to industrial enterprises, and those enterprises had to strive for profit in order to repay the government, with interest.

From those examples, it seems that all productive and distributive endeavor was profit system effort. That effort was hampered by the dictatorship hanging like a mill-stone around the necks of the workers. Can we lie to ourselves by believing that this was pure nationally owned production and distribution?

Various "state enterprises" used the State Bank as the go-between on transactions between those enterprises. For example, perhaps as tractor stations bought tractors from the tractor factories, money had to pass through the State Bank. Should this be interpreted as showing governmental ownership and operation of the tractor stations and factories? Or was it checking on the flow of money so the government knew amounts of money changing hands?

The State Bank collected taxes and other state income. I have found no specific reference as to who paid taxes. Under all of the adverse conditions, maybe it was still posssible that individuals had enough income to pay some type of income tax. Maybe only the cooperative enterprises had to pay taxes. But if these cooperative enterprises belonged to the government, why should they pay taxes to that same government?

Existence of taxation makes it seem like the government did not operate cooperative enterprises, but shifted responsibility to cooperative groups. My bet is that somehow the eventual source of the taxes was the individual worker, like the farmer getting decreased pay because the collective was taxed.

Long lines of shoppers always existed trying to buy food at stores that were woefully understocked. This is difficult for me to understand, so you may get little help, here. Looking with eyes used to seeing profit system problems that are symptoms of deficiency of buying power, it is a puzzle to see Soviet people with buying power unable to find enough food for sale. Hidden in the Soviet dictatorship, there must have been some obstacle to the flow of money from consumer to store to bank to collective farm. Did the money get diverted to factories producing military hardware? When the government set the prices to be paid for the quota of agricultural products, were the prices so low that the manager of the collective farm could not keep workers, nor rent tractors, nor pay taxes, etc.?

Low agricultural output is my symbolic example of all Soviet low production in goods for consumers. Although covered by Soviet secrecy, there was a decline in goods needed by the general population. This decline worsened as the years went by. We have blamed most of this situation on dictatorial mismanagement. Maybe those managers were also working with actual profit system processes badly tangled by cumbersome bureacracy.

Going beyond governmental mismanagement, it seems beyond belief that the farm workers where not intelligent, not strong, not knowledgeable about farming, or otherwise incapable. Could it be that the workers deliberately were unproductive? Could they be unproductive to the point of endangering their own survival? It is my belief that you should not blame the workers for lack of production.

Lack of worker incentive could stem from non existence of profit motive or from passive opposition to the dictatorship. Many economists in the United States, and many other people, will swear that the profit motive is necessary to force people to work. Such a belief ignores the many millions of wage earners in the United States, people who work hard but never expect to be profit receiving business owners. Yet you, the reader, will need to think deeply about the profit motive for you are faced with the decision to sink with the profit system or develop a non profit alternative economics system.

My wife firmly states that she would refuse to work if she was alongside of some "lazy, no-good idler who was loafing on the job". She feels that most other persons would loaf if the means of production and distribution was not privately owned and operated by an economic dictator who forced people to come to work and to perform. In words from the above paragraph, "the profit motive is necessary to force people to work". "Survival motive" is a phrase that is rejected from conversation. How many other people are there who think survival motive is not important alongside of profit motive?

Was the lack of profit motive the killer of worker incentive in Stalin's Soviet Union? My guess, and it has no real proof, is that passive, unaware resistance to dictatorship increased almost imperceptively over the years until each person joined all other people in low output. If all the depressing effects of dictatorial mismanagement, fear, guilt associated with condonement, etc., are put together, the presures could perhaps squelch personal incentive to the point of endangering survival. It appears to me that the lack of incentive for the massive population was not self created, but was psychological destruction of people by a dictator. This seems a failure of dictatorship, not a failure of the workplace.

My search in this chapter was to find success and failure of Soviet Communism, with reasons why. The picture that has emerged so far shows that Soviet Communism was a faulty hodge-podge that was partly publicly owned enterprise and largely profit system private enterprise. Looking at the Soviet mishmash, it does not seem that real public ownership of production and distribution ever had a chance to perform. We know that the Soviets used profit system procedures, and know those lead towards eventual permanent depression. We can also see that few Soviet individuals seemed to get rich. Any profit was likely "farmed back" into the system in a manner that minimized the profit percentage rate.

Soviet Communism could be compared to a very large single business system with a near zero profit. Such a system would only slowly move towards permanent depression. In spite of many appearances of profit system methods, a near zero profit rate was too low to be responsible for Soviet Communism's failure.

Looking at the economic design, the actual economic operations of Soviet Communism appear to be rickety enough, haphazard enough, that collapse could easily occur. Because of the economic jumble, it is hard to lay one's finger on exact causes of economic failure, except for the clear-cut blame that rests on dictatorship. Even after empty stomachs of consumers had long proven economic failure, the dictatorship refused to admit it.

Joseph Stalin died in March of 1953. A chain of dictators followed Stalin. Those will not all be named, here. Through the years, as Soviet dictators emerged and disappeared, the truly significant policies did not change. The population increased to 300 million people. Nearly all lived at a level barely above starvation. They lived in fear, with the degree changing a bit as different dictators were in control. Also, the cold war continued, with nuclear warheads numbering into the thousands.

Finally, one of the dictators, named Mikhail Gorbachev, broke the pattern. He ignored the hostile words often said by United States President Ronald Reagan, and heard the few words of peace that

Reagan thought it was his role to say. In spite of the predominance of hostile words, Gorbachev made the first move of disarmament, and also talked openly to the Soviet people about talking openly. Emboldened by Gorbachev, other Soviets began to move towards irradication of dictatorship. Forced by Gorbachev's peace moves, President Reagan began to distrustfully copy the Soviet peace moves. The tide had turned for Soviet Communism, and in August of 1991, major breakup of the Union of Soviet Socialist Republics began. Before the year of 1991 ended, the United Soviet Socialist Republics ceased to exist except as past history. One great sadness is that the people of the one time Soviet Union may greatly undervalue the world leadership of Gorbachev. Perhaps the run-of-the-mill, down-to-earth United States citizen appreciates Gorbachev's brave and far sighted actions more than does the people of his native country.

Here is a huge warning to the people of the former Union of Soviet Socialist Republics. In your shift to a "market economy", to a profit system, you are picking up a poisonous snake and holding it to your chests. Embrace democracy, most certainly, but never again confuse a political system with an economics system.

(Reader note: the above paragraph was written six years ago for my first edition. Today, the year is 1998, and Russia has disasterously tried the "market economy". Severe exploitation occured.)

All through this chapter, one of the

important implied questions has been, "Would people make an adquate effort to produce in an economy not motivated by the attempt to make profit?" An inadequately motivated effort by the total work force would doom publically owned production and distribution, leaving the people subject to famine. Through sev- several pages, both the implied and stated answer was that people would work, shown by the amount of production for the military in the last few years of Stalin's dictatorshsip. Considering the conditions of dictatorship under which the Soviet people strived, it is amazing that there was much obvious accomplishment.

My book implies and states that the dictatorship part of Soviet Communism exerted an unending detrimental effect on the Soviet people's effort to feed themselves. I have said that dictatorship physically crushed peole, emotionally and psychologically distorted them, and stole the bread out of their mouths by diverting production to military purposes.

In the United States, some percentage of the people seem to believe just the opposite of my presentation of Soviet Communism's failure. Those people say that dictatorship is necessary to force people to work within publicly owned production and distribution, and that people would simply starve without a slavemaster, or a profit motive for incentive.

Following, in this paragraph only, is a condensation of some opinions sometimes appearing in United States newspapers: The state in the Soviet Union, practically free of charge, provided food, clothing, housing, medicine, education, jobs, and old-age pensions. The state ran farms, mines, electrical power plants, transportation, factories, construction, communication, department and grocery stores. For this benevolence, the state demanded practically nothing from the citizens. Because this cradle to the grave cushy social structure did not motivate the citizens to effort, the economic system was a failure, and the nation's pride had to be salvaged by the creation of one of the world's greatest military machines. Some people believe this view, and I believe it wrong.

People's feelings and beliefs about any social system are important. Feelings support opposing conclusions even though derived from the same general conditions. It would be wonderful if some clear proof existed showing that a non-profit system used by hundreds of millions would be workable. To my knowledge, there is no example which can be pointed to, saying, "Here is a large scale, non dictatorial, high living standard public enterprise that proves to anyone that public enterprise works. It is a shining example of utopia brought about by publicly owned production and distribution, with no master using whips, clubs, guns or secret police. It is a democracy that has evolved to the minimum of force against individuals, etc." Such utopia has not yet been contrived. People can only assume that it may be possible, or partly possible, having looked at the error of dictatorship which seems to have been the main cause defeating Soviet Communism.

I believe that in chapters one and two of this book there is clear proof that the profit system will permanently collapse, world wide. People can only hope that we can contrive a successful non-profit system to replace the failing private enterprise profit system. My strongest advice is that we must avoid dictatorships.

There is another very significant lesson to be learned from Soviet Communism. Be aware of the speed at which disintegration of the Union of Soviet Socialist Republics took place. If you people, the "masses" in the world, decide that you must improvise a non-profit system, do it long before chaotic conditions occur from profit system collapse. For millions of people, perhaps a billion, to establish any new social order, requires their widespread awareness and planning as far in advance as possible.

Chapter 5.
Towards the Horizon

"Why are you hitting yourself over the head with a hammer?" one man asked another.

"Because it feels so good when I stop," replied the other man.

Jokes are jokes, but many hide real wisdom in nut meat form. I think it is time that people actually quit hitting themselves over the head with dictatorship or with an economic system which is mathematically self destructive. "And so," you ask, "what do we change to?" The start of the answer is that we must begin the new design by excluding the most painful and destructive economic and political methods of the past. We must look without blinders at history, then quit hitting ourselves over the head with a hammer.

We, the people of the United States, are faced with an extremely difficult choice. Other people who currently use large scale private enterprise for profit have this same difficult choice. The profit system, which we used for so long, is finally failing, and its failure will be final. Dictatorial public enterprise has failed, and collapsed, in the Soviet Union. Dictatorial public enterprise has failed on a human rights basis in China. There is definitely no certainty that a workable and humane democratic public ownership can be contrived, let alone become accepted by enough people to get it established. We are between a "rock and a hard place", between an impossibility and uncertainty.

If we decide that uncertainty is preferrable to impossibility, that we will try to design production and distribution that is publicly owned, it should become a "do it yourself" project. Letting a dictator do it for you will sandwich mankind in between two impossibilities; the failed profit sytem and the sure to fail public enterprise controlled by a dictator. Only if you "do it yourself" in order to guarantee democracy will the new social order have a chance for success.

My input of suggestions in this chapter are all do it yourself suggestions, regardless of how strongly they are supported by me. My suggestions are not a blue print to be rigidly followed. Be wary of anyone's suggestions if those are offered as rigid blue prints. This is necessary to avoid dictatorship. Now, almost a contradiction, it seems most important that dictatorship be rigidly avoided. If you do not avoid dictatorship, you won't need to hit yourself over the head with a hammer for long. A dictator will do it for you.

And so, as you people forced into creating a new social order begin your plans, make sure that all parts of the plan foster democracy, not tyranny. Start making those plans during a period of peace and minimum amount of duress. Read, and study, and talk with each other. Welcome controversy, but only controversy in ideas, not in violence or suppression.

Welcome democracy, using law to limit and to delegate authority. The Constitution of the United States is a pattern stating the population's supremacy over all delgated authority. That essential part of the Constitution should be meticulously retained, but amendments will need to be made to allow for changed economic procedures. All of those changes will require the greatest possible participation of the population, and will take time.

It is a definite shock to think of the need to alter the Constitution, although this can be done by amendment. It implies a finality, a certainty that need exists for massive and very careful work. If enough people learn the basic system analysis of the profit system, and become convinced that permanent depression is impending truth, then a new econmic and social system will be developed.

To avoid war, to avoid dictatorships, we need to carefully select economic processes. An economic process is very potent in controlling economic and political possibility. For instance, if something is bought or made for one dollar, and then sold for one dollar and ten cents, the process becomes impossible if used large scale over a long time. How could such a simple two step process be anything except innocent? How could it possibly lead to aggressive search for foreign markets, maybe war, or the social chaos of permanent depression? But that simple two step process, if analyzed within system law, shows that it will bite the hands that feed it. As you people design a new economic system, check the simple details of design, making sure the procedures will not boomerang and fail, or give tyranny.

Small activities may determine major possibilities, as well as force behavioral trends, or patterns of life. Avoid profit systems procedures, even on a limited scale. For instance, handcraft work can be exchanged by barter, but not sold for profit. Apples raised on a family's back yard tree can be traded for an oil painting by a local artist, but not sold for profit. International barter can be undertaken, maybe trading wheat for oil, but the first time that someone buys the wheat for one price and tries to sell it for a higher price, the ultimately impossible profit system is being used. So be careful, and shun profit system procedures.

Many of the subjects that are considered in following paragraphs will necessarily be presented like jig saw puzzle pieces. Most subjects will be quite incomplete, and you will need to assemble the pieces into a growing total picture in your mind.

Present day money has many useful qualities, part of which can easily be kept by a society using publicly owned production and distribution as a way of living. Present day money, and money in ancient days, allowed someone to carry something small yet exchange that for something that was bulky or heavy. In ancient days, the usefulness of money as a "medium of exchange" was the prime purpose of money. An adequate substitute for this medium of exchange capability can easily be contrived.

Another very useful quality of present day money is that it gives people freedom of choice (if they have money). Consumers purchasing at a store are "voting" for the type of goods the consumer wants the store to restock. You hadn't thought of it as being a daily vote that controlled both production and distribution? It is. We want a newly contrived economics system that responds to the daily wishes of the consumers. If you wish to name this "democracy in the market place", you are probably right.

Today, as the check out clerk moves the consumer's purchase over a scanning device full of electronics, the exact nature of the purchase is recorded. On a daily basis, if desired, other electronic devices itemize and summarize all of the purchases, forming the basis for reordering stock to replace items purchased. Here we see an example of how small activities control major procedures. Continuing use of these methods in a new economic system will allow consumers to control all consumer goods distribution. The next link in the chain is that distribution, summarized, can be the basis for requisitions which will control quantities of production. Please note that there is no need for some individual tyrant who makes decisions for the consumer population, forcing quotas on the population, giving them a glut in some things and a scarcity in other things.

The realities of production capability places limits on how much the consumer can take home in a set period of time. This, not a dictator, dictates the need for some limitations on how much the consumer can "spend". The limitations of reality, the determination of consumers's limits, should be done by a group of people who are under controls exercised by the entire population. You, the do it yourself designer of a new social system, should watch this limit setting activity with a cautious eye to avoid the start of tyranny.

People who estimate how much total production the nation is capable of in perhaps one year would also estimate how much of that would be available for consumer use during that same year. Merely for example, we could assume that each consumer could spend $35,000 per year during the first year, or maybe it would be $53,000 instead. During that year, a new estimate should be made to establish consumer limits for the next year. To me, it would seem wise to have tentative determinations for a few years in advance. All of this is not new and strange, but is merely use of the budgetting which every family, and every nation does somewhat well, or poorly, today. We should be aware that the amount assigned to consumer use would be only one portion of the total budget, with other amounts assigned to agriculture, transportation, education, etc.

To allow for realistic setting and resetting of limits for consumer spending, unused "money" should expire at the end of the issue period. The same expiration process should apply to allotments for all other national budget items, such as agriculture, transportation, etc. This would seem necessary to allow accurate determination of the amounts of the next issue.

A pre-determined amount of "money" should be issued to every citizen, merely because every citizen exists. Argue extensively if you wish about this next suggestion. The expiring money to which each citizen is entitled should be the same for each citizen, adjusted for infancy, childhood, adulthood, and comcompleted family raising, but not according to type of work and skill. To give some one the authority to set different levels of money entitlement according to type of work and skill is to leave a huge gap asking for dictatorship to insert control. Also, recall that little procedures can have long lasting effects, and some may have very deep and somewhat unexpected side effects. The necessarily complex establishment of work titles and "pay" values would create a stratified society. It would also take up a great deal of work hours, and bring endless controversy between workers and "pay" setters. Beware of petty tyranny, for tyranny defeats accomplishment, and tyranny always builds empires.

There is a very strong further reason why pay values and work titles should not affect income. Starting with the industrial revolution, before the United States became a nation, the relative value of individual labor began to be outmoded. In today's mechanized industrial world, one machine can outwork hundreds of laborers. For example, one earth moving self-loading scraper capable of a seventeen cubic yard load can move more dirt than a couple hundred men equipped with shovels, picks, and wheelbarrows. It is machinery that gives us our standard of living, not how many man-hours of hand labor is involved.

To keep the "money" in the hands of the person to whom it is issued, the "money" should not be in the form of dollar bills, fives, tens, twenties, etc. That form of "money" could be stolen from the rightful owner, or it could be hoarded by large groups and spent in a sudden demand for goods, destroying the planning necessary to periodically issue new "monney". The form of the money, quite different from our present "paper currency", could be like our present "plastic money", very familiar to anyone who has a credit card. With modern electronic accounting methods, each person could be given his (her) own account from which to draw.

Each use of today's credit cards incurs debt, and causes the debt to be recorded. The name, "credit card" is therefore not proper for a card to be used by the future consumer. Perhaps a new title like "spending card" is much better for a card used for recording expenditures from a person's "wealth" account. The remainining balance can easily be established with modern electronic computing and record keeping. With each use, the card would identify the account, and with other identification, would tend to insure against use of a stolen card.

For some individuals, there could be a tendency to binge buying, fouling a personal budgeting plan. Also, during change over to a new economy, it would seem likely that many people would buy a huge amount and hoard it. Perhaps once a year setting of the amount to be issued to each citizen would give sufficient time for planners to establish the amount available. If this yearly amount was divided by twelve, each part issued to the citizen's account once a month, the binge spending would be lessened for the few persons addicted to binge spending. Unused monthly balances could accumulate for one year, then expire if unused.

The subject of binge spending and hoarding was brought up for a couple of reasons. First, it was to imply that there are a lot of details to setting up a publicly owned economic system. Second, it was to raise the idea that there might be a great deal of misgivings about the system as it is first put into operation. It would seem to me that this initial insecurity would be unavoidable. It could be minimized by planning for transition, with retention of old familiar operations only slightly modified. For most people, the use of a personal account card would be a change, but an acceptable amount of change, even though people today seldom use a "credit" card to buy groceries.

Feelings of insecurity about a new economic system should depend upon the degree of stability of the procedural design which you people contrive. Feelings of security will also be influenced by recognizable logic in all procedures, perhaps allowing easy acceptance of something which is a bit new. For instance, buying groceries with your personal account card would be a bit new, but an easy step because it is logical, little different from paying today with a check.

In preceding paragraphs, there are suggestions for possible procedures for distribution of consumer goods to consumers. Next to be considered are some suggestions on ways in which production procedures and other necessary activities could be organized. The use of departments to put together activities that are alike has long been used. For example, it is suggested that there be a department of transpostation. That department should be broken down into sub departments. For example, one of these should be railroading, another should be aviation, another should be highways, another should be trucking, another should be automobiles, another ships and boats, etc. The department of aviation should be further broken into passenger transport, cargo transport, and general. Such organization by departments has a long history of use, and has proven itself.

Putting democracy into each department is merely a matter of arranging control so that all the people affected by decision making have control of the decisions. In different words, management should be responsible to those managed, plus management should be responsible to the public.

Making management in a single department responsible to those managed is quite straight forward. For example, assume that in an automobile factory, a foreman is needed on an assembly line where a particular stage of frame work assembly is done. Choice of that foreman should be done by all of the workmen who are part of the crew doing that particular assembly. These are people who are daily aware of the activities where they work, aware of how the work crew inter relates. The supervisor who works with several foremen along the assembly line, who in present day useage would be called the "boss" of those foremen, should also have a "vote" in choosing the replacement foreman. That supervisor, supposedly an expert, should have a "weighted vote" worth more than the vote of individual crew members of the assembly line. However, the supervisor should not have a weighted vote that outnumbers those of all the crew who will be working with the new foreman.

Women, use of the word "man" anyplace in the foregoing, or any place within this book, is purely a writing convenience, not implying that the word "woman" could not replace the word "man".

In the selection of a supervisor who coordinates the work of several foremen, also apply the rule that management be responsible to those managed. That means that members of many crews and many foremen will vote to select the supervisor who coordinates work of several foremen.

We can easily see that it would not be useful nor necessary for the assembly crew on a particular stage of frame assembly to "vote" for a foreman working with the people who paint the car body. However, if the manager of the entire factory needs to be selected, all assembly crew people, all painters, all information handlers, etc., should be involved in selection.

It is unnecessary to wait until some pre set calendar date called "voting day". The needs of the work-a-day world could control the time when voting should occur. And how about term of office? Periodic times could be set for the general public to either retain departmental managers or to require replacement. This could be the manner in which the general public could exercise control over any department, so that the "foxes would not be the only ones guarding the hen house."

The above methods would very likely place democracy in control, but also introduce what might be called use of "mass brain power." Everyone working in a department would be contrtibuting to management. The need for labor unions would be eliminated, in my opinion. It is expected that you do-it-yourself social system designers will thoroughly review everything above, modifying it in ways you might feel are needed.

There is more to a social system than just production and distribution. Most of these other needed activities could readily be arranged by departments. Let me mention only one to be the example of all. Music, very much a useful art for any society, is very creative. There are doubtless a multitude of other activities that society would desire to have included into the mainstream of those functions supported by our entire nation. These should be formalized, and become recognized departments.

The way in which the different departments relate to each other needs a lot of your thought. If there are too many rules established, some activities could be greatly hampered. If no rules are established, a lot of rivalries grow, with duplication of effort. If you think for a bit about the present day relationship between various "departments" of our military system, you have good examples of the need for cooperation between departments where public ownership is the way of life. (Yes, today the population of the nation owns the military services).

Let's consider an example of how different departments might need each other. The highway department needs dirt moving equipment. Assume you have established a department specifically for earth moving, with bull dozers, big scrapers, back hoes, loaders, trucks, and a myriad of other types of equipment. Perhaps the prime purpose of this specific department is to do dirt work for flood control, or to do the dirt work needed for large developments for housing. Should the highway department also have equipment that duplicates that of the earth moving department?

Recall that in the rigid dictatorship of the Soviet Union, cooperation between "departments" was conspicuously poor, and avoid rules that restrict departmental cooperation. It is my suggestion that you let your departments overlap each other somewhat, and also allow them to give each other much support. There will be an over all job to accomplish, that of working for the nation.

How about "funding" for departments? It seemed rather easy to contrive "funding" for consumers. We could simply give every citizen a share of the "funds" available for that purpose. "Funding" some departments could be just as direct, resulting from decisions of the planning people who would allot part of our nation's production capability to some departments. For example, the highway department could use a certain portion of the nation's potential. Just like a citizen with an account on which to draw, the highway department could have an account on which to draw. The allotment into the account of the highway department should expire at the end of the period for which the allotment was planned.

The preceding straight forward funding for some types of departments seems simple enough, but look at the direction in which decisions point. Compared to the total population of the nation, the people who would make up the group deciding allotments would be a tiny minority. This tiny minority group would be making decisions that would effect 200 million people. Also, the subject of the decisions is one of the most important in the nation, the nation's yearly budget.

It would seem highly desirable to place this tiny group of decision makers under control by periodic election. Perhaps half of the group could come up for election each two years, with a term of four years. That would give an overlap of experience, but tend to stifle the tendency towards dictatorial decisions.

Funding of departments making consumer goods might be slightly more complex than the funding of departments such as the highway department. Let's split the problem into two parts. First, there are decisions to build stores, consumer goods factories, and other supply sources. That could be done just like funding the highway department. Second, complete control of production, transportation, and distribution at stores should be controlled by consumer spending.

It might seem that the preceding paragraph is full of much ado about nothing. There are some objectives to be accomplished, though. Flow of consumer goods should not be full of disruptions and delays. Remember the Soviet Communist stores with barren shelves that resulted from dictatorial centralized planning which placed consumers at the bottom of the list. Centralized planning can be very useful, even necessary, if daily procedures of commerce place consumers in control of planning and eliminate dictatorial control. The flow of consumer's "plastic money" on a daily basis needs to be the method for the consumer to control both production and distribution of consumer goods.

Perhaps we can trace what could be a typical flow of activities, starting with a consumer. Assume a man chooses a pair of shoes at a shoe store. The check out would result in reading the code for the pair of shoes, and the reordering of a replacement pair just like the ones purchased.

Funds for store operation should come from the consumer's payment for goods. Next, the shoe factory should be given a major portion of the "payment" made by the consumer at the store. This portion of the cost of the shoes could be applied by the factory on the cost of raw materials and factory operation. In this way, the shoe factory could operate on a combination of funds, those allocated directly by the planners, and those coming from consumer choices. Transportation of the replacement shoes should be funded from the payment made at the store.

No funding should in any way depend upon making profit from any stage of the total sequence of operations. There should be no "loans" involved. When the funds from the consumers have served their purpose of controlling production, the funds should expire, having accomplished their goal.

An effort has been made here to come up with a possible method to place maximum control in the hands of consumers and eliminate the need for decisions by sideline planners.

Today, when people go to work for a private business concern, their boss, or supervisor, likely is witness to the amount of time spent at work. Perhaps the worker is required to keep a record of his work time.

There would seem to be little need to set up a new method for public ownership workplaces. It is unlikely that people in general fear that workers would fail to appear at the location of their work, with that attendance accounted for in appropriate records. It is somewhat probable that large numbers of people might feel that workers might report to work, but refuse to do any significant work.

For hundreds of years, people have become deeply accustomed to the idea that some people must force other people to work. Now, we are faced with the idea that people might, or might not work if they are "paid in advance" by a personal "bank account" given to them just because they are citizens. All of our lives until now we have been aware that people seemed to labor only when necessary for their survival. Can we now go against all of our lifelong observations and expect each worker to work just because he is a citizen? But, survival is involved.

Very strong logic tells us that each person supposed to work must work or else the new publicly owned economic system will fail from the very start. Very strong logic also tells us that if our new publicly owned economic system fails, we will have no working economic system, since the impending permanent failure of the profit system will destroy our privately owned economic system. Will logic prevail, or will we all sit on our behinds until civilization collapses into chaos, and starvation gets us all before we can recover?

It is my prediction, perhaps naive, that people will avoid hitting themselves over the head with a hammer. When, and if, we establish full public eeconomy, the people reporting to work will discuss the needs of themselves and their nation, then in growing groups will commence working. This is my belief only if we avoid all use of dictatorial pressure at the job site. If dictatorial force is exerted to require work performance, we will completely lose work performance as subconscious opposition to tyranny grows into group approval to refrain from work.

Once again, the most studied and strongest effort should be made to design daily work customs which completely exclude the creeping growth of dictatorship in the workplace. Creative thinking is not easy while being flayed by a cat-o-nine tails. Hidden rebellion and work decrease is the product of tyranny. Don't beat ourselves over the head with a hammer by compromising with force to get labor.

All of us today are jointly the heirs of the industrial revolution and of all industrial achievements since then. Before us, we have a tremendous opportunity. To harvest that opportunity, we can not abstain from work when we should work. The rewards can be very great if we join together in willing cooperation to operate the industrial machinery that has evolved almost to automation. Cynical though we may be, is there not some strong expectation that capable workers will work when the incentives are so positive?

How about the people who have handicaps that make them less productive than those who can fully produce? To answer that question, remember that "no man is an island." Regardless of how gifted and capable you may be, you are incapable of self support in the style which is possible from a cooperatively operated modern industry. To operate that modern industrial machine, there is definite mutual dependence between all of the workers. Each capable worker will need to rely on every other capable worker to jointly operate that complex and potentially very productive industrial gift which is our mutual inheritance. We should not exclude the crippled, or otherwise handicapped person, from joining in the operation, refusing them the sense of accomplishment and self esteem earned by their perhaps limited contribution. Neither should we in any way forget that those people are also joint heirs of the knowledge and equipment developed by our forebears, entitled to equal benefits along with the most capable person.

It may help us have an over all perspective to incorrectly say, "The vast capable work force can, with the aid of modern industry, produce a wealthy nation." Let us reverse that statement, to make it correct. "Modern industry, with the aid of the vast available work force, can produce a wealthy nation." From that statement, let us restate two important points. It is machinery, not "manpower", which can produce abundance for us. Because machinery does the real producing, we can and should let all people benefit, even those totally incapable of being part of the work force.

With a national work force of 100 million, or more, there are going to be people who wish to change types of jobs. There are going to be people who wish to live in other parts of the nation. With such a numerous crowd, countless opportunities will exist for workers to exchange places with others who also wish to have job mobility or geographical mobility. Simple rules that strongly avoid dictatorship should allow mobility.

As we consider farmers and agriculture, it might be timely to state something only implied so far. A major portion of all property should be owned by the entire nation. The shoe factories, the railroad locomotives, the distribution stores, etc., should be public property. So should be the farms.

During the past several generations, possibly no group of workers in the nation has worked harder, nor longer hours, than farmers. Generations ago, farming was a family business, with fourteen hours of work per day a very common occurance. Often, the work force was the family members. In emergency conditions, that work force responded any time of the day or night. Economic dictatorship was very minimal, and self reliance and independence were often maximum. Their farm land and agricultural equipment tended to be privately owned by each farm family. Probably no group has been more essential to the welfare of the entire nation.

In recent decades, farming became increasingly capitalistic. It became necessary to have increasingly expensive tractors, harvesting combines, trucks, gang plows, buildings, etc. "Hired hands" were more often necessary to augment the labor of the farm family. With all of these changes, another change occured. Farm families started to be massively in debt, with increasing amounts of the farm earnings diverted to paying interest on loans. More and more, farms ceased to be owned by the farm family, with banks and other financial instituutions holding dominant behind-the-scenes ownership. For a large portion of farms, change to public ownership someday will not be "loss of the farm" by the family that has labored so long to keep the family farm going. The farms already are lost by many present day farm families.

Perhaps agricultural department organization will re-instate the farmer back onto the land even more so than the present day bank owned farm allows. Perhaps the worker who chooses to work the publicly owned farm soil will be able to do so without fear that he will be displaced from the work he loves.

It should not be too hard to define the line between future public property and personal property. The word, "personal", rather than private, starts to set up a logical division. A person has exclusive control of personal property.

The idea of who has control also helps us define property. A house which is rented, today, is owned by some landlord, but renting gives a few exclusive privileges to the renter. The renter has limited exclusive privileges to use the house as a home in which to live. The renter's personal property can be stored in the rented house. Such personal property as clothing, beds, etc., are under full control by the renter, and the landlord who owns the house has no control over the renter's personal property. The landlord can not enter into the rented house, nor use or take the renter's personal property.

The renter may not modify the house except in ways that the renter and landlord have agreed upon. The renter and landlord may have an agreement about the length of time the renter may stay without the landlord repossessing his house, evicting the renter. There seem to be clear differences between private property, such as the landlord's house, and personal property, such as the renter's clothing.

There are clear differences between public property and personal property. There are also distinct differences in use of public property, depending upon who has control. For example, it may sometimes happen today that a person rents a house that is owned by the national government. In that case, the renter may place his personal property in the publicly owned house. However, there is a difference between who uses the publicly owned house and who has use of a public park playground. The general population may use the public park, but the general population does not have use of a publicly owned house rented by some individual. Agreement about who has control over the use of property, public, private, or personal, is what defines property. A piece of paper that declares "ownership" of property may be far less important than an agreement about who has "use" control.

In a society based upon public ownership of production and distribution, there should likely be no private ownership of any real estate, including houses. There should be use agreement about private control of publicly owned property, agreement so firm that the person who rents a publicly owned house can say, "My home is my castle." Ever family in the nation should have exclusive control of a home even though the house and grounds upon which it sets is owned by the entire nation. That rented control should continue unless relinquished by the family.

Geographical permanence and geographical mobility should be made equally the rights of a family. At the present time, with private ownership of homes, geographical mobility is often hampered for months or years because of inability to sell a home in one area and at the same time buy a home in a distant location. Within a public economy, mobility might exceed what is possible with private ownership of real estate. With rented homes, either staying in any area or moving from it should be easily accomplished since we would have the population of the entire nation to give flexibility.

The design of a publicly owned economic system can include rules that give renters rights that nearly coincide with the rights of today's private ownership. There should be differences, such as no renter should be forced to live in a rented two room hovel while someone else lives in a twenty room mansion. The equality of each person's yearly "income" should take care of that, with a family having numerous children able to "afford" a bigger house than one rented by a childless couple. Remember that all children should have an "income" account. Parents acting as trustees for their children can use their children's income to supplemnet their own when renting a house big enough for a large family.

It is my belief that if you do-it-yourself social system designers do your job real well, you can define rented public property in such a way that future renters have more rights and security than those presently given by private ownership.

This book will not try to make a list of types of property that should be personal property, what should be rented public property, what should be open access public property, what should be public property under control of public departments. You readers can sort all types of property into categories to fit your desires if you merely define use rights for each type. Perhaps rented public property should include homes, horses, automobiles, boats, smaller airplanes, etc. Perhaps emphasis should be placed on open access public property, such as parks, highways, etc.

With all homes being rentals, home mortgages would no longer exist. Neither would there be any need for loans, not just for real estate, but any where within a publicly owned economy. For emphasis, recall that the Soviet Union had a governmental bank, and loans. This was mentioned in an earlier chapter as a probable mistake in economic procedure, because collecting interest was a private enterprise profit system action still remnant in the middle of supposed public enterprise. It also had attachments to tyranny, with some one within the dictatorship having decision control about who received loans. Do-it-yourself economic system designers can eleminate the loan and interest collecting process from publicly owned economy. It is an anachroonism needed only in a profit system and as a method of dictatorship.

As the loan process is eliminated, we can also eliminate banks, a profit system institution based on loans and collecting interest. Banks have been with us for two thousand years, but we owe them no reverence beyond saying they once served a purpose.

The true source of national income is the quantity of energy available to the nation from oil, coal, hydroelectric water power, nuclear power, wind mill power, bio-mass heat output plants, geothermal plants, solar power collection, etc. To a tiny degree, horse power, oxen power, "manpower", and so on, are also sources of the total useable energy within the nation, but so negligible and incapable of determination that we should not even count it. Gold that we dig from a mine or pan from a river does not determine our living standard unless we foolishly allow it to control distribution, and thereby control production. It is the total energy available within the nation that sets our living standard capability, and the income of the nation during any one year should be set by how much of that energy we decide to use in any one year.

In a truly publicly owned economy, the "government" has no need for taxes. (To me, major property in the Soviet Union was not publicly owned, but instead was dictatorially owned. Recall that taxes were collected in the Soviet Union.) The idea that taxes are not necessary takes a bit of getting used to. For example, you do not have to tax the population to get "money" to build a hydro-electric project. Engineers and other technical people estimate the amount of energy sources within the nation. Other engineers estimate the cost in energy to build a particular hydro-electric project. Planning people merely assign a portion of the nation's energy resources to the project. This need only be a book keeping procedure.

It is significant that debt based money would not be needed in a publicly owned economy in which the energy sources of the nation form the base for the nation's living standard. Compare that to the profit system's need for debt increase at a compound profit rate to enable the profit system to function.

Taxation to attempt debt repayment, resulting in removal of buying power from the system that demands buying power increase, will pass away as the profit system passes. Additionally, the debt based buying power of the profit system bears no true relationship to the availability of energy sources, nor national resources. The profit system's demand that we use energy sources and resources at a compound rate will pass away with the profit system. A publicly owned economy that bases its living standard expectations on the actually available energy will be far more in tune with nature than the profit system is.

It is possible to both dispense with taxation and greatly diminish the role of what we today would consider to be governmental activity. The "government" in a publicly owned economic system might have a few other duties, but largely should be a custodian which allocates energy expenditures to various projects. Since mere book keeping forms a large portion of this activity, the "government" workers who do this need be little different from the information handlers at a large factory. Never the less, as mentioned many pages back, some budgetary duties make the work of the energy allocating people nationally important. The general public should have ultimate control over these budgetary people.

Using a publicly owned economic system, you need not fear that abundance will cause system break down. Recall that in a profit system, productive abundance that could not be sold happens when the buying power pool is too low to absorb the abundance. Recall that this brings firing of workers, waiting for stored goods to be sold, although the sudden increase in unemployment brings no increase in buying power. Hence, the profit system's paradox of increasingly poor distribution and consumer hardship when production began working best.

In a publicly owned economy, there would be no procedure causing an endless effort to take more cookies out of the cookie jar than are in it. In a publicly owned economy, a surge in abundance would mean that production had actually surpassed consumer need. Production could be decreased to match consumer need without disrupting the economy, nor causing consumer hardship. Abundance is entirely acceptable in public enterprise, and will not destroy the economy.

Before picking up the next subject, let us return to one that is many pages back. Some of the paragraphs just before this one paint a rather rosy picture of abundance in an economics system in which the public owns everything except personal property. Let us not forget that a core question is whether or not the workers will actually work in the kind of public economy just portrayed.

Let us not forget that Soviet Communism collapsed amid obvious signs of workers not working even when poverty was rampant. Let us not forget that Soviet Communism was a very viscious tyranny, so intense that subconscious rebellion likely took the form of ineptness at work and utter minimum job output. Also, let us be aware that the daily economic procedures within Soviet Communism were quite different from those portrayed in preceding paragraphs and pages of this book. And let us not forget that the future of the profit system offers only economic collapse.

The Soviet citizen who abstained from work had begun to believe that his country could switch to the "free economy" and "free market" of capitalism. Maybe, if the Soviet workers had known that a mathematical problem was going to sink the boat of capitalism, they definitely would not have planned to switch to capitalism. Those workers could have beaten the dictatorship by letting the system collapse, then set up a democratic public enterprise economy. Maybe they would someday produce at work and thrive, free of the tyranny which was the most likely cause of the collapse of Soviet Communism.

Now that we have again brought up the real uncertainty that workers will work without a profit motive or a whip, we can consider the feelings of present day very, very, wealthy people. It would seem that they may be quite reluctant to trade their positions of superwealth for the nebulous promise of assured abundance in an economy where the mass population owns everything except personal property. Let me admonish every reader of this book. Do not forget the tragic mistake made by Vladimir Lenin, who thought that people had to be forced at gun point to change economic systems. Remember that dictatorship, once entered into, is a one way street to total subjugation and destruction of even the loftiest of goals.

Give everybody in the United States, including the very rich, a chance to look at simple cookie jar arithmetic and change economic systems because of solid logic. Even though there is great risk of chaos if change to a new economic system is delayed too long, give people time to observe the increasingly severe early-warning rumbles of profit system failure.

At the opposite end of the wealth scale, very far from the secure rich person, are the unemployed people. These people in daily jeopardy may think that it is an asinine question to wonder if workers would work in a publicly owned economy. Even those workers still partly supported in the safety net of unemployment insurance would seldom hesitate to trade unemploymnet insurance for full employment, even at a laborious job. This willingness to work applies even more strongly to those unemployed who have used up their short-term safety net.

More than the safety net support of unemployment insurance sustains vast numbers of unemployed people. Even when they are unsure of getting their daily bread, most still believe that politicians can repair some mysterious broken part of our profit system, making the system work well from then on. But if you listen, there are definite doubts that our present economic system will give our children and grandchildren all that it gave in years long gone. Those rumblings of doubt are just part of the increasingly severe early-warnings of eventual profit system failure.

Perhaps a great majority of the population will follow up their doubts by an insightful study of economics, and determine that politicians are powerless to reverse the mathematics evident in cookie jar law. Here lies our hope for a future of survival, and probable abundance.

Maybe a difficult, but essential job, should be accomplished by do-it-yourself social designers. You need to assure freedom of the press in your new economic system. We may grant that the rugged individual print shop owner who printed newspapers at the close of our Revolutionary War has long been displaced. We also know that "press" today includes radio and television as a means of disseminating information. We also know that these "media" are subject to the viewpoints of ownership by necessarily wealthy people. Yet, in the future economic system, you must build "freedom of the press." To start the ball rolling, it is my suggestion that we modernize the wording in our present First Amendment, and say "freedom to publish information."

A possible method of attaining freedom of information is to set up a department for that purpose. Within the department would be people who would operate the "machinery" of news gathering and publication of that news. In addition to the publication of news, there should be publication of a forum of ideas and opinions by anyone who wants to stand up in "the town hall" to "speak his piece."

There needs to also be provision for publishing books.

So far, in this chapter, examples of the most important procedures, both economic and political, have been presented. You, the reader, can make a list of requirements to be met by your future society, and a list of essential services you might expect to establish, with methods outlined to achieve those goals. Following is a list that has occured to me. This example list is certainly not complete. It is presented along with the idea that you, the population of our country, will "carry the ball" as soon as you are convinced that you should.

Included in my list, there should be a constitution defining both political activities and economic structure. The constitution was mentioned earlier in this book, but is repeated as being very important.

An essential responsibility of the new society is conservation of the natural resources of the nation. Merely as a single example, there should be a shift to windmill electrical power generation. There could be some amazing conservation advantges for a nationally owned economy where duplication of effort is eliminated, and the greed level of the profit attempt is gone. But, this conservation will not work with a dictatorship, neither political nor privately owned. You must have both political democracy and a nationally owned economy. The goal to be followed then is that people must be cared for, but environmental exploitation beyond that is rejected. Wouldn't you like to replant forests full of oxygen producing trees, and do it on a national basis?

Control of pollution is basic to conservation of our resources. In the United States, acid rain has killed forests. In the Soviet Union, acid rain was far worse than here. Granted that we did not know, once, about some forms of pollution, like acid rain. Now that we know, we must stop, not just acid rain, but all kinds of pollution. Our survival on this planet is tied to how we handle our environment just as it is tied with the need to establish a new economic system when the profit system fails.

Speaking of the necessity to care for the population, you are going to come face to face with the problem of the "population explosion." Often times, the population tends to be a positive exponential growth. If you look back at the end of Chapter 2, finding the graphs of compound profit, you see the manner in which population growth tries to occur. However, the growth rate in the United States is far lower than it once was, and this proves that the explosion can be contained.

The population, all ages, needs medical care. You say you already had that responsibility on your list? Good. Establish a department. Enable medical people to take on all kinds of staggering challenges, like building a defense against that civilization threatening disease, Auto Immune Deficiency Syndrome, known as AIDS.

An educated population joins nicely

with research and development to increase the living standard of the nation. We need a department for education, and one for research and development.

Expect change, which is inevitable, and ever more rapid. This is an older man's lifetime observations giving advice.

There can be great optimism about mankind if we escape from jungle law. We have strong jungle law mixed in with love for our neighbors, with jungle law a present day necessity in our lives. It has threatened to sink civilization, but jungle law can be removed from the scene when we sluff off profit system ethics. Our real enemies are not other people, but hunger, lack of housing, lack of medical attention, etc. Instead of wasting time grabbing at each others throats, we can work in cooperation and accomplish some of our dreams. It could become possible that we will have to increase the size of our dreams. Let other nations imitate.

The often repeated question about whether people will work or not in a publicly owned economy seems to me quite insignificant when compared with another question. Need there be war?

That question is worthy of an entire book, and many books have been written on it. In this present book, many causes of war will be passed by, leaving only a very brief consideration of the economics causes of war and the results of dictatorship. In earlier parts of this book, international economics pressures were thought to be seeds of war. In our profit system, the investors within our nation invest 500 billion dollars and need to sell 550 billion dollars worth of goods. Our internal market can absorb 500 billion dollars worth. The remaining amount, 50 billion dollars worth, represents the amount that investors call their profit, if they can find a market. That is why a profit system economy needs to find and exploit foreign markets. Exploitation of a foreign market pushes us towards war, especially if the foreign nation is trying to exploit us as its foreign market.

In a publicly owned economy, there is no unsold surplus representing profit, and no need for foreign markets to exploit in order to sell that surplus. This greatly reduces the economic pressures towards war. Here we see a very strong positive reason to establish a publicly owned non-profit system economy even if the profit system was not going to self destruct.

Our publicly owned economy should have a department specificly for international trade. That trade should be based on exchange of goods. Many pages back in this book, it was said that no profit attempt should be made during the exchange of goods. There should be no attempt at exploitation of another nation.

Don't believe that eliminating economic pressures will get rid of all causes of war. Even religion has caused wars. Also, there are always some people who thirst for control over other people. Dictators and war go together. First comes the dictator, then very probably, war. How can you plan a democratic and productive society if you have war? War must be avoided, but how?

There is a pattern as dictators take control over other people, whether this is in a neighborhood gang, or subjugation of a nation. Make no mistake, there is power in the methods of dictators. At the start of dictatorship, any power the dictator has is increased by the subservient attitude of the dictator's victim. If the dictator is allowed to dominate, it may soon become impossible to remove the dictator, or avoid obeying any wish of the dictator, including war.

Peaceful people say, "We declare peace." Violent people reply, "We declare war." Declared war destroys peace. That is why violent people so often seem to have full control of whether there is war or peace.

Dictators hand guns to peaceful people and say, "You are now soldiers. There are enemy soldiers who will shoot you unless you shoot them first." Enemy people are told the same. That is how violent people entrap peaceful people into war.

War is extremely wasteful of people and things. Wars tend always to get bigger and more intense, beyond anyone's control, not stopping until all of the things and people have been used up. After the fighting is over, there are angers, hatreds, and fears from which new wars start. Turning loose this unstoppable destruction is the most stupid thing people can do.

Someone who stands up in the middle of battle and shouts, "Stop this stupid nonsense!" can't be heard above the noise of war. Even if soldiers could hear, each is afraid to stop, fearing that a soldier on the opposing side will kill him. The peacemaker is apt to be mistaken for the enemy. "If you are not for us, you are against us," fighters fear. The war trap stays closed, and is even glorified as patriotism.

Can there be no hope of getting rid of war? It is possible. When there is war someplace, there are also many places without war. There seems to be far more peaceful people than violent people. Yet it is in times of peace that do-nothing peaceful people fail peace. During times of peace, war makers organize for future war. During peace, if we organize strongly enough for future peace, we might make it lasting. Until we do, we are condemned to fight, trapped by tyrants.

Start by working to rid ourselves of economic pressures towards war.

The structure of this book has been sparce framework rather than blanket coverage of everything. The frame tends to be a wheel, but with many missing spokes. At the hub is systems law, the cookie jar, and futile attempt to take more out of a system than is in it. In different words, the hub is the profit system attempt to break system law. The spokes included in the wheel are a few of the system's failures, all symptoms of the disease, which is the hub. Also included as spokes are some of the shenanigans by which people have tried to make the profit system give more than is invested.

One such attempt to make the profit system work has been growth of debt inserted into the system to increase buying power enough to realize profit. Inability to indefinitely insert debt at a compound rate will cause full failure of the system.

Another spoke in the wheel is the effort to find markets external to the system. This can not be acheived because nationally internal markets and external markets are all internal to the profit system enclosed by the Earth.

Another wheel spoke was ordinarily known as business competition. Related to that spoke is the forced antagonism between business and labor. When we follow other nearby spokes, we have profit system ethics, in which people forced long enough to live by jungle law nearly lose all feelings of concern for other people.

Innumerable spokes can radiate from the hub which represents the ultimate futility of the profit system. People continually bump into spokes, such as unemployment. Each spoke is explainable by application of the basic theory found in Chapters 1 and 2. The complete array of all spokes, all malfunctions and successes of the profit system, were far beyond the scope of this book. The ones in this book were chosen as perhaps the more important examples.

One subject which was not a spoke of the wheel was mixed in with the subjects that were spokes. Democracy and dictatorship considerations were freely applied throughout the book. It was claimed that each could be teamed with either the profit effort or with public ownership of production, distribution, and services. However, dictatorships will certainly destroy either private economies or public economies. A public economy will be workable only if it is teamed with democracy.

Using cookie jar law and the profit attempt as a base for understanding bedrock economics, this book has partly presented a democratic publicly owned economic system that would seem useable by mankind when the profit system fails.

What are our chances? Is the future a matter for pessimism or for optimism? We have become so accustomed to the roller-coaster action of the private enterprise profit system that we look with unnecessary trepedition to change that we are forced to make. People will persist and survive. Any direction they take will involve struggle, and there will be cost, but effort and intelligence will prevail.

So far, this chapter has presented some of the desirable design features of a public enterprise free of tyranny and possessing maximum control by the population. Yet, a very important problem has been cheifly ignored. How do we get there from here?

Minimizing chaos during transition is extremely important because chaos carries with it two very undesirable features. One is that the population of the entire country will suffer hardships, even starvation and extreme violence dependent upon the degree of chaos. The second undesirable feature is danger of incipient dictatorship developing during chaos.

Transition must be a major part of the total design. That transition should be based on three important factors. One factor is the imperative nature of making the transition. That has been considered through the the entirety of this book, but needs to be reemphasized, now. No person, no political party, can stop the results of the built-in design of the profit system. We are forced to try a non-profit system.

The second factor is the need for a preparatory design completed in at least tentative form prior to the forced transition. This preparatory design must be based on mass awareness of true economic cause and effect. The design must be free of dictatorship and democratically acceptable to the majority of the population. Only the involvement of the huge majority of our population can make that publicly owned economic system work.

Third, there can be no expectations of individual survival unless it is supported by group survival for the great mass of people.

You social system designers have some staggering challenges, but they can be inspirational, too.